# The Challenge to Scholarship

**What does scholarship mean?**
**How has it come to shape the structure of higher education?**
**What should its role be?**

Discussions about the nature and role of scholarship have a long tradition – from Aristotle to Boyer – and the term is often perceived as complex and ambiguous.

At the same time, determining what 'scholarship' stands for is critical, as it is a concept central to the function of higher education and influences higher education practice and policy throughout the world.

*The Challenge to Scholarship* is a lively and engaging investigation that seeks to establish what it means to be a scholar and the value of scholarship. It addresses current concerns and tensions including the scholarship of teaching and the relationship between teaching and research.

Gill Nicholls gets right to the heart of the debate over scholarship and declares that a reconceptualization of scholarship within universities is required, outlining the changes involved and the practical implications for higher education institutions of the future.

**Gill Nicholls** is Professor of Education and Director of King's Institute of Learning and Teaching at King's College London. Gill has extensive research experience and has published widely. She is also involved in consultancy work evaluating university learning and teaching strategies and learning and teaching research strategies.

# Key Issues in Higher Education series

Series Editors: Gill Nicholls and Ron Barnett

*Books published in this series include*:

*Citizenship and Higher Education*
edited by James Arthur with Karen Bohlin

*Defending Higher Education: The Crisis of Confidence
in the Academy*
Dennis Hayes

*Universities and the Good Society*
Jon Nixon

*The Challenge to Scholarship: Rethinking Learning,
Teaching and Research*
Gill Nicholls

# The Challenge to Scholarship

## Rethinking learning, teaching and research

**Gill Nicholls**

Routledge
Taylor & Francis Group

LONDON AND NEW YORK

First published 2005
by Routledge
2 Park Square, Milton Park, Abingdon, Oxon OX14 4RN

Simultaneously published in the USA and Canada
by Routledge
270 Madison Avenue, New York, NY 10016

Transferred to Digital Printing 2006

*Routledge is an imprint of the Taylor & Francis Group, an informa business*

Typeset in Palatino and Zapfhumanist
by Keystroke, Jacaranda Lodge, Wolverhampton
Printed and bound in Great Britain
by TJI Digital, Padstow, Cornwall

*British Library Cataloguing in Publication Data*
A catalogue record for this book is available from the British Library

*Library of Congress Cataloging in Publication Data*
Nicholls, Gill.
   The challenge to scholarship : rethinking learning, teaching, and
research / Gill Nicholls.
      p. cm. – (Key issues in higher education)
   Includes bibliographical references ( ) and index.
   ISBN 0–415–33532–9 (hardcover)
   1. College teaching.  2. Learning and scholarship.  3. Universities
and colleges—Faculty.  I. Title.  II. Series.
   LB2331.N52 2005
   378.1′2–dc22                                    2004014255

ISBN 10: 0-415-33532-9
ISBN 13: 978-0-415-33532-4

November 25 2008

*In memory of my Father, who taught me to challenge, question and learn*

# Contents

*Preface*                                                                    ix
*Acknowledgements*                                                           xi

**Part 1  Establishing the concept of scholarship**                          1

1   Why challenge scholarship?                                                3

2   Historical concepts of scholarship                                       9

**Part 2  Policy and power: influences on scholarship**                     33

3   Policy and initiatives: the need to reconceptualize
    scholarship                                                             35
    *Simon Lygo-Baker*

4   Scholarship of teaching: an emerging concept                            55

5   Disciplines and scholarship: challenging the power                      73

6   An international perspective: the implications of
    scholarship for professionalism                                         93
    *Simon Lygo-Baker*

**Part 3  Challenging the future**                                       **111**

7   Scholarship: the challenge of the future                        113

8   Scholarship: a hostage to fortune                               133

9   Final comments                                                  139

     *Bibliography*                                                 143
     *Index*                                                        157

# Preface

As this book goes to press the Higher Education Bill (2004) is being discussed in parliament. The consequences of the bill can and will have far-reaching consequences for higher education, from the number of students that will be going through the system to the expectation of professional standards related to teaching within institutions. Each one of these elements causes change and a small change in one area can cause a catastrophic change elsewhere in the system, as chaos theory demonstrates. How will these changes affect the scholar and scholarship within the academic community and particularly those who are involved with, and passionate about, teaching and learning?

The role of teaching, learning and scholarship has been brought to the forefront of debates within higher education as the enhancement agenda has gained pace. Within this agenda a variety of approaches to enhancement have evolved. The predominating arguments are related to the notion and concept of the scholarship of teaching and the implications this has for the learning community within higher education.

The scholarship of teaching introduced by Ernest Boyer (1990) captured the imagination of all those involved in the learning enterprise in higher education, but had particular impact on those involved in educational development and the enhancement of learning and teaching in higher education. Interestingly, the notion of the scholarship of teaching has had global interest and impact. Originating in the USA, it has transformed itself across the world.

This book considers, examines and questions the development of the term 'scholarship' and challenges the notion of scholarship within the context of a changing higher-education environment. The context of the challenge is based on the premise that the very term 'scholarship' currently has multiple meanings and interpretations, and that this multiplicity has caused confusion within the higher-education community and has not always helped the cause of enhancing learning and teaching. The challenges to scholarship faced by the academic community are considered from a variety of perspectives, internationally, nationally, generically, philosophically and on the basis of individual disciplines. The aim of the book is to provoke questions and discussion within the community and thus open further the ideas and challenges to scholarship, scholarly work, learning and teaching.

# Acknowledgements

I would like to thank Steve Jones of RoutledgeFalmer for the opportunity to write this book and include it in the series Key Issues in Higher Education. Steve's support throughout the writing of the book has been significant, and his patience and sustained humour have been key to its final publication.

I would also like to thank Simon Lygo-Baker, who has contributed to this book, not only academically but through his continued moral support. Thanks are due too to my team within KILT, whose ideas and comments have always been helpful and perceptive. To the staff and colleagues in King's who helped with the research on which the book is formulated. To Harry Musselwhite, whose continued support enabled the book to be written. To Stuart's sharp eye for detail and finally, but not least, to my family, whose support was immeasurable considering how little they saw of me whilst the book was being compiled.

*Part 1*

# Establishing the concept of scholarship

*Chapter 1*

# Why challenge scholarship?

> Every word has a meaning. This meaning is correlated with the word. It is
> the object for which the word stands.
>
> (Wittgenstein)

Wittgenstein in his early writings believed that 'Every word has
a meaning. This meaning is correlated with the word. It is the object
for which the word stands' (Wittgenstein 1953: 1). It is the application
of the word that provides the meaning: the context that is given
or associated with it. However, as John Locke suggested over three
centuries ago, knowledge and understanding are often held back
by words that have no fixed signification. As a result a term can appear
beset with controversy and debate because of an unacknowledged
ambiguity in how it is applied. Could this be the case with the general term 'scholarship' which no longer has a fixed significance? If so,
we would expect the result to be controversy and ambiguity whenever
it is applied.

Our understanding of a general term extends beyond one individual
thing to those that share common attributes. For example, the word
'car' includes every car that has ever been or ever will be in the world.
The intention of such a general term is that it suggests a set of features
that are shared by everything it applies to – in the case of 'car', perhaps
'a wheeled vehicle designed for transportation'. As a result, for
Wittgenstein words are like tools in a toolbox. Their functions vary
according to how the speaker wishes to use them. Their difference is
what makes them useful and gives them authority in each particular
situation. When an individual reports to another upon the meaning of

'scholarship' the goal is to inform that person of the accepted meaning of the term. This is a 'lexical' definition because it is a simple way of replicating how the term is already used. The definition becomes accurate depending upon how well it captures the usage of the term at that moment in time. The key element in meaning is the understanding of the word by those using and hearing it. But as Wittgenstein suggests, it is the circumstance that surrounds the use of the word that gives it the meaning each time. This suggests that meanings change and that the universality of language is fluid. This may provide us with clues as to the interpretation of the word 'scholarship' both over time and also within different environments. If scholarship as a concept is to have meaning to and for the academic community and the society that scholars serve, then it needs to be understood by how it relates within the world that is observed.

This book considers how the meaning associated with scholarship has altered over time and to do this examines the contexts in which it has changed. It considers the lexical definition, and how the general term 'scholarship' has been extended, to create an understanding of the common attributes that it denotes. From here it becomes clear that the context within which this definition gains its meaning has grown increasingly complex. It can be viewed from different perspectives: within an occupation, for instance, or within a particular location or language. This suggests that understanding of the term 'scholarship' within the academy in the USA, the UK and Australia (for example) will differ because of the qualifications used. As the postmodern state becomes an ever more complex set of overlapping structures and cultures, these qualifications become ever more diverse. For human beings attempting to predict outcomes this increased complexity is discomforting. The result is an attempt to set a common and accepted context within which meanings can be identified. In the case of scholarship this attempt was initially undertaken at a disciplinary level, where shared 'professional' values provided the basis and context. However, there is an increasing literature that suggests that the individual institution's context now prevails over the disciplinary and it is from this that the individuals now draw their shared values. If this is the case it clearly has implications for the conceptualization of scholarship, both as a term and for the definition of what this word actually means. As the original meaning of scholarship has changed or developed, the qualifications against which it becomes understood have increased so that a universal understanding becomes increasingly unlikely.

As the meaning of the general term 'scholarship' has become increasingly context driven, one response has been the adoption of a new, more specific, term that has not previously existed in the academic's language: 'the scholarship of teaching'. The scholarship of teaching had no existing standards, and the goal since Boyer (1990) has been to propose the adoption of a shared use for this new term. Achieving agreement would significantly reduce the vagueness of the general term 'scholarship' by providing a clearer and sharper explanation of a related concept. This book attempts to provide a view on how the term 'scholarship' is already used within higher education and then considers whether or not the notion of the scholarship of teaching sharpens our understanding of this by removing the vagueness that has built up over time.

In an ideal world, academic scholarship would not need to be defined or encouraged. It would arise naturally from the intellectual curiosity and energy of the academic community at its best. But in the real world scholarship has been subjected to an elaborate system of rewards and punishments created by the higher-education community. The consequence has been that academics have been encouraged by the needs of these systems to find an aspect or interest within their disciplines, i.e. a scholarly niche, so that they can keep up with professional dialogue, and join in the scrutiny associated with their disciplinary community. The push towards the scholarly niche or specialism continues as the information available on disciplines increases and the authority of the academic becomes more overtly questioned. In addition to this the higher-education community expects that the scholarship produced will make a significant contribution to the field of knowledge engaged by academics, but the contribution must also be personally and professionally renewing. A large demand from a concept termed 'scholarship'!

## The structure of the book

The main theme of this book is scholarship, its meaning and its place within the academic community, and the extent to which its meaning has changed and influenced the thinking that has occurred within higher education. Its aim is to challenge traditional thoughts, ideals and ideologies, as well as the epistemological grounds on which scholarship is discussed and used within the community. Each chapter deals with a specific issue, by identifying the central points of debate and linking them to possible ways forward. The book is divided into three parts, thus identifying the main areas of debate and influence.

The first part deals with setting the context and exploring the historical and philosophical aspects that have led higher education to conceive scholarship in the way that it is currently interpreted. Chapter 2 traces the historical development of the term 'scholarship' by focusing on the nature of the term and the contexts from which it has emerged. Aristotelian and Socratic philosophies, as well as the ideas and beliefs of John Henry Newman, offer theoretical under-pinnings for the examination of the term. These are then taken further by considering how the emergence of research became a university goal and as a consequence of the changing objectives of the univer-sity the term 'scholarship' slowly but definitively took on alternative meanings within the academic community. The argument is further developed to show how, with the changing goals of the university, scholarship needs to be considered as a learning activity – but in reality became and continues to become more detached from learning – and the implications this has had for the student and the academic. At the heart of the discussion is the need to understand the epistemological grounds and underpinnings on which academics as individuals and institutions collectively base their assumptions of learning and under-standing. The premise is that what academics think they believe is not always what they practise. Hence epistemological examination has become a key ground for discussion and a possible avenue for the redefinition of scholarship. However, for academics to understand why it is necessary to investigate epistemological frameworks also requires them to engage with what the purpose of scholarship is, could be or should be. This leads into a discussion of the ideas connected with scholarship and the scholar, and argues that the boundaries around the scholarly enterprise should be drawn more widely and allow for the development of knowledge in a more open way – one that creates interest rather than narrowing down the avenues of enquiry.

The final elements of Chapter 2 deal with scholarship and the ideals of education, considering the philosophical works of Socrates, Plato, Dewey and Kierkegaard. It suggests that these philosophies give us an insight into why the ideals of education focus on learning and rationality, and that universities need to consider learning as a core function for both students and academics. This last element is what has currently caused conflict in understanding scholarship within a fragmented framework of research versus teaching. The cause of the perceived conflict is examined from the perspective of promotion and tenure and the implication these have for scholarship and the role and behaviours of academics within higher education.

The second part of the book relates to the introduction of the term 'the scholarship of teaching' within an educational development framework. Chapter 3 concentrates on the policy and power relationships in the development of the term 'scholarship'. Three aspects are given significant attention. The first relates to principles and reasons why policy initiatives aimed at enhancing teaching and learning in higher education should make reference to the concept of scholarship. Within this framework several key issues are raised, such as the importance of values in understanding and defining scholarship, the nature of policy in influencing such values, and the need to reconceptualize scholarship. In an attempt to expand the questions that should be asked of scholarship, the nature of excellence is considered and used to show that although it has gained currency within higher education it is not always a useful term when trying to define concepts. The final commentary relates to the urgent need within the community to collectively reconsider the term 'scholarship' and to take back control of the definition.

Chapter 4 argues that the term 'the scholarship of teaching' has become confused and misplaced within certain communities and used to sustain and enhance a particular type of credibility in activities related to the enhancement of learning and teaching in higher education. Bourdieu's concept of symbolic culture is used to construct the argument and shows how the use of the term 'the scholarship of teaching' needs to be re-examined and conceptualized. The argument is reinforced through a piece of empirical research that considers perceptions of the notions of scholarship and the scholarship of teaching among twenty-five academics from a variety of disciplines. These perceptions are examined in the light of disciplinary style and behaviours as well as generic elements of belonging to an academic community.

Chapter 5 relates to the nature and influence of the disciplines within scholarship. It concentrates on trying to understand why and from where the disciplines have gained their power in higher education and the reasons why they maintain such prominence. Defining a discipline is a starting point for the discussion, as is the need to answer the question 'why consider the disciplines in a debate on scholarship?' The notion of specialization and territorial boundaries within and between the disciplines is also considered. These debates shed light on the role of the individual within the discipline and how this influences action taken by academics. Fear and risk are key notions within the arguments put forward. Particular attention is given to the work of Palmer. No discussion about scholarship within the disciplines would be complete without an exploration of disciplinary styles: ways of knowing within the disciplines, and the influence these may have on teaching and learning within the disciplines. Finally, issues around power and change are considered and are related to why disciplines remain such a firm institution within higher education.

The third and final part of the book concentrates on international perspectives and the challenges scholarship has to face in the future. The nature of international perspectives, and the influence these have had globally, cast an interesting light on the concept of scholarship. Although each continent has been researching and questioning the term 'scholarship', and in particular the scholarship of teaching, each has developed a different perspective and angle on the problem. We try to show that although it is essential that we share our findings, the findings cannot be assumed to be transferable. Each community has considered the scholarship of teaching within its social and cultural context, and as we have argued throughout the book, social and cultural aspects underpin the very nature and conceptualization of the status and positioning of scholarship within the respective higher-education communities.

Challenging the notion of scholarship is like any other academic challenge. There is a need to consider underlying theory, historical and sociological perspectives and alternative avenues that might shed light on the issues and questions related to the concept under investigation. Challenging the notion of scholarship has uncovered an array of perspectives including fear, risk, complexity and power which have proved both fascinating and in urgent need of attention from the education community. It is hoped that this book expands and increases the questions and the dialogues which will ensure that the challenge to scholarship proves worth while.

*Chapter 2*

# Historical concepts of scholarship

Teaching is the highest form of understanding.

(Aristotle)

The concept of scholarship is often traced back to the Greeks, for whom scholarship and character went together. A proper patriotism and the worship of the gods were virtues esteemed in the ancient world. 'We must', said Plato, 'assimilate ourselves to God, seeking to become like him, wise and just and holy.' To mould the character of the young, he said, 'teachers are enjoined to look at the child's manners even more than to his reading and music', and the only education which truly deserves the name is 'that education from the youth upward, which makes a man eagerly pursue the ideal perfection of citizenship'.

In his classic work *The Idea of a University* John Henry Newman set forth the notion that the purpose of the university is to promote and disseminate knowledge. Since that time, the concept of scholarship and the promotion of scholarship have belonged to academia. Scholarship can be said to be at the heart of the professions and higher education. There is little doubt that nothing brings greater honour to an academic than a reputation as a scholar. For most in higher education, the concept of the scholar and scholarship are nearly synonymous with the role of the academic. Thomson (1996) suggests a lexical definition of a scholar as 'a learned person, especially in language, literature, etc.; an academic' (p. 910). Similarly, scholarship refers to 'the methods and standards characteristic of a good scholar' (p. 911). Certainly there are scholars who do not teach, but scholarship is recognized as the fundamental qualification for most academic positions within universities.

Newman's definition of the university is important in relation to the discussions on scholarship, scholars and a community of scholars. Within this discourse Newman suggests the ideal of intellectual culture as a means to explain the nature of learning within a university. He argues that the best aid to professional and scientific study is for the

> man who has learned to think and to reason and to compare and to discriminate and to analyse, who has refined his taste, and formed his judgement, and sharpened his mental vision, will not indeed at once be a lawyer . . . or an orator, or a statesman, or a physician, or a good landlord, or a man of business . . . but he will be placed in that state of intellect in which he can take up any one of these sciences or callings I have referred to . . . with an ease, a grace, a versatility, and a success to which another is a stranger.
>
> (quoted from Cameron 1978: 145)

Newman, a man who could be said to have 'a high tolerance for restatement', laid out an idea of a university that excluded research, locating discovery and the advancement of knowledge in separate academies and confining the university function to teaching. Newman's 'idea' of a university has significant associations with the past while simultaneously assimilating and expanding a collegiate ideal of his own. He described the purpose of the university as the diffusion and extension of knowledge rather than its advancement. If its objects were scientific and philosophical discovery, 'I do not see why a University should have students'. 'Lest the learned world become stagnant' (Cameron 1978: 1), he recommended that other bodies – institutes or academies – should be devoted to the creation rather than the dissemination of knowledge. Newman was content to leave research to research societies, what we might call institutes or think tanks. Newman firmly believed that 'To discover and to teach are two distinct functions rarely found in the same person'. It is interesting here to note that George Orwell abandoned teaching because he later observed that, despite appearances, teaching and writing do not go together. Orwell described teaching as a semi-creative activity and one that siphoned off just enough energy and time to make serious writing virtually impossible. Orwell was not a university teacher, but was making the same point as Newman. This continuous distinction between teaching, research and scholarship defines Newman's work and consequent interest in his thinking surrounding teaching and the university.

Newman's pedagogical principles have been written about widely, but most contentious have been his views on research within the university context. Pelikan in *The Idea of the University: A Re-examination* (1992) considers Newman's ideas about university research. He expresses a deep admiration for nearly all of Newman's pedagogical principles except for this one issue. Pelikan states that the four legs of the university table are:

1. the advancement of knowledge through research
2. the transmission of knowledge through teaching
3. the preservation of knowledge in scholarly collections
4. the diffusion of knowledge through publication.

Pelikan argues that no one of these legs can stand for very long unless all are strong. As it is the omission of research, in particular, that is today the target of reform polemic – and he cites Charles Sykes's *Prof Scam* as a typical contemporary indictment against the so-called soft-headedness of researching professors – Pelikan opposes the case that universities have become nothing more than teaching institutions. If such a thing were to happen Pelikan states that the university as we know it will be threatened. But why is it that the university of today focuses on research rather than scholarship?

## The emergence of research as a university goal

The university in its present configuration is essentially a German creation of the nineteenth century. Research was a hallmark from the beginning. Ringer in his book *Fields of Knowledge* (1992) shows clearly how the German model of university education comes into existence and how and why it was adapted in France and Europe. University research was perceived by the Germans as having a considerable advantage for the practical and technological futures of German society, but the theory underpinning this view was not merely utilitarian. The theory aspired to the sublime; this is encapsulated in one of Germany's eminent scholars, Adolf von Hamack, when he argues the case for a research mission:

> Never must our German universities and institutions of higher learning change their character of being devoted both to instruction and to research. It is in the combination of research and instruction that the distinctiveness of German institutions of higher learning is expressed; but this distinctiveness, in which research and instruction mutually fructify each other, would be completely destroyed if this combination were dissolved. . . . In some countries the chief emphasis lies on introducing students to the results of scholarship. But at our universities we want to introduce them to scholarship itself, and to teach how one arrives at the reality and truth of things and how one can advance the progress of scholarship. In other words, students must be taught the how of scholarship as well as the what.
>
> (Ringer 1992: 45)

Such views were powerful and important to the university sector both in the rest of Europe and particularly in the United States, where academic sojourns in German universities throughout the 1860s and 1870s by scholars such as Bancroft and Eliot stimulated the adoption and adaptation of the German philosophy of higher learning. The German university was considered to be a haven of pure research, the main ideal behind it being that the university could be a seat of learning where pure scholarship and enquiry were encouraged, where professors were free to pursue their research without hindrance or interference.

Ringer (1992) notes that Prussia's success in the Franco-Prussian war of 1870–1 was a decisive event in university education, as its victory was widely perceived to be as a result of its superior educational systems, particularly at the university level. As a consequence of these events the German university model and views of research and scholarship gained considerable appeal. This was particularly evident in France, where Durkheim led the fight for the modernization of the university curriculum and for institutional alterations that would enable France to compete with Germany in higher learning, research and scholarship. This process was replicated with variations throughout the Western world, but its purest replication has been in the United States, where research dominates the social and cultural essence of the university structure.

# The changing concept and meaning of scholarship

Following the emergence and embedding of the German model of higher learning and university experience in the late nineteenth century, the question of what scholarship is and in what forms it manifests itself began to dominate the discourse of the twentieth century and the notion of scholarship began to contract, particularly in the sciences. With the explosion of the information highway the scholar can no longer maintain intense familiarity with all spheres and sections of intellectual activity. The contraction of the individual's personal boundaries of scholarship has resulted either in intense or restricted specialization or in more shallow learning over broader areas of knowledge.

William Whewell over 150 years ago argued against such contraction of scholarship by suggesting the concept of 'consilience', a notion that has recently been revisited by Wilson (1998). The essence of consilience is the testing of theory by coincidence of inductions derived from different 'classes of facts'. Embodied in the concept are possibilities for:

- the application of a broader scope of scholarship than is usual in the practice of contemporary disciplines, and therefore
- a more substantial validation of knowledge.

It is a shame that Whewell's views have been ignored. Instead, specialization can now be traced to the increasing demands of funded research and the gaining of funds to support research programmes. This in turn has increased the need for productivity through the publication of journal articles and the dissemination of the research enterprise. To some in academia, particularly in the sciences, the pinnacle of scholarship and possibly the very definition of scholarship has become synonymous with peer-reviewed papers and blue-chip research funding. These have over time come to be seen as scholarship rather than possibly the products of scholarship; in other words there has been an equating of scholarship with research. This process has further contracted the concept of scholarship, and scholarship is increasingly evaluated on the basis of research alone rather than a variety of activities that are part of the scholarly process. The equation of scholarship solely with research has ignored the fact that scholarship is inherent in the intellectual substance of all communications of the scholar, whether they are journal papers, textbooks or undergraduate classes (Gibbins 1998). As a consequence, the definition of scholarship within universities has evolved and certain operational aspects have become attached to it. As Dirks (1998) suggests, 'the measure of one's scholarship is the fundamental criterion for all meaningful rewards in colleges and universities, including retention, advancement, prerequisites and recognition. Over time the focus of scholarship, and thereby its definition, has become quite narrow and increasingly has been seen by the public as irrelevant to society's goals for higher education' (p. 1). Currently in higher education 'to be a scholar is to be a researcher' (Boyer 1990: 2).

The rising dominance of the research role is evident in the very notion of research-led higher education. The evidence suggests that in 1969, 21 per cent of all faculty members in the USA found it difficult to obtain tenure without publishing. By 1989 the figure had doubled and in 2003 the number had trebled. Comparable figures are found in Europe and the UK. For academics a focus on research, where knowledge is constructed, takes the lead over teaching. It is clear that within the late twentieth and early twenty-first centuries 'research culture' has become the dominant force in higher education. Within this context there has more recently been an increased interest in redefining scholarship. However, if this is to succeed there has to be a recognition that a change in academics' understanding of epistemology is required.

## Scholarship as a learning activity

Scholarship has recently been considered as an activity, a practice, a calling, a responsibility, a privilege and a necessity, that is endemic to the professional life of an academic. It often seems curious to those in the outside world that academics spend time thinking about the concept and notion of scholarship. However, the cornerstone of teaching is learning, and of learning, reflection. Reflection on the topic of scholarship has a simple purpose: to think about what it is we are doing as scholars, teachers and academics. What are academics doing with the opportunities, challenges and responsibilities in their collective worlds, in service to their students and colleagues, their universities, professions and communities?

In higher education, if academics are at all successful as teachers, they have a passion for either scholarship, teaching or research, and have found a way to transfer that energy from one to the other. There are, however, times in an academic's life when these elements need to be rediscovered – when he or she needs to reawaken the desire to know. This requires time, imagination and the reconnection of interests with questions and a passion for learning. Aristotle suggests that by nature human beings desire to know, that critical enquiry first begins with wonder. An academic's primary incentive is to rediscover his or her discipline through scholarship. 'As such, scholarship can be thought of as a condition of the intellect. It is complex and requires the exposure of knowledge, its validation and its examination. Scholarship identifies the missing links in – and denies the boundaries of – the multidimensional lattices of knowledge. It seeks new intellectual perceptions, opportunities and directions. It nurtures creativity and uses it synthetically in the furtherance of understanding. It is a progenitor of wisdom' (Gibbins 1998: p. 47). Gibbins suggests that

> the concept of scholarship is discipline-independent. It applies equally validly to science, to the arts, to the humanities and to other intellectual endeavours. Importantly the description invokes no particular means whereby scholarship is to be displayed or recognised. This omission is deliberate because scholarship can be, and is, reflected in all human intellectual activities, and arguably none has greater claim to validity as a vehicle for scholarship than any other. The issue of validity rises with respect to scholarship, not its vehicle. Thus no particular form of expression of scholarship can be seen as being a defining element of scholarship; neither can it be dismissed as being irrelevant. Nonetheless, the expression and communication of scholarship, by any means, are crucially important to both the collaborative development of ever-wider scholarship and to the maintenance of its generational continuity.
>
> (Gibbins 1998: 1)

Shulman (1999) contends that for an activity to be designated as scholarship, it should manifest at least three key characteristics: it should be public, susceptible to critical review and evaluation, and accessible for exchange and use by other members of one's scholarly community. Thus all forms of scholarship can be considered to be acts of mind or spirit that have been made public in some manner. Scholarship properly communicated and critiqued serves as the building block for knowledge growth in a field. Many who wish to extend the notion of scholarship to teaching activity within the university accept Shulman's view, and by so doing raise both the status and value teaching has within the community. This particular concept is discussed in detail in Chapter 7. However, within the present discussion it is interesting to see how Shulman's view can add to the debate about scholarship as an activity for learning.

Gibbins (1998) argues that equating research with scholarship is often reflected in the manner in which the scholarly activity of academics is evaluated: 'Like teaching, research is also a process, and like teaching, to be meaningful, it has to be predicated on sound scholarship. It must also be contributive to it by providing new and appropriately validated information' (p. 2). Gibbins's perspective on epistemology suggests that a redefinition of scholarship which integrates teaching and research would be of significant benefit to a more unified approach to learning. Rice (1996) argues that what the academy needs is a complete scholar, one who would have a sense of the ways in which different forms of scholarly work interrelate and enrich one another, and would be capable of moving with ease from one scholarly task to another: 'The tensions between connected knowing and analytical capabilities, on the one hand, and reflections and active practice, on the other, would be nurtured and built upon rather than resisted and minimized' (p. 22). This argument puts learning at the centre of the discussion about scholarship. Lynton (1995) sees an important value in the integration of professional service and applied learning with formal cognitive learning. He takes the view that in professional programmes, the clinical components in the traditional approaches only serve to apply classroom learning, and argues that knowledge often emerges from the complexities and rigours of practice. Knowledge is 'dynamic, constantly made fresh and given new shape by its interaction with reality. Its application constitutes learning for the scholar, arising out of his or her reflection on the situation-specific aspects of the act of application' (p. 7). These values are very important, not only for the individual scholar, but for the institution itself. 'The integration of professional learning into instruction should be an institutional goal – giving professional learning legitimacy and importance as an institutional priority' (Lynton 1995: 16).

Both Gibbins and Lynton are arguing for an appreciation of the various forms of learning and teaching that might constitute scholarship. Within this argument it is clear that the nature and purpose of scholarship within learning is still not well established, either for institutions or the individuals within them. Considering scholarship as a learning activity brings into play a variety of contexts and concepts such as power, identity boundaries and individualism. Many of these will be discussed throughout the book. Here it is important to raise the issue of power, and recognize that power cannot be omitted from any discussion of learning or teaching. As Jarvis (1992) explains, 'however democratic or pluralistic society appears to be, the process of control or influence occurs in every society and organisation and affects everybody's consciousness. The extent to which this happens in various societies differs. But it is clear that these processes are related to learning that takes place in society and organisations' (p. 87).

The notion that learning is the focus of organizational processes and that the individual within the organization has a need to participate in those processes reaffirms that a clearer understanding of the purpose of scholarship is required. The individual's need to know and learn can form a fundamental argument for scholarship as a learning activity. A basic assumption about academics and those involved in the academic world is that they have a wish to know and an interest in learning. Although the concept of interest plays less of a role in learning theory than the concept of need, the two concepts are linked, and help identify alternative understandings of learning activities and scholarship.

Jarvis (1992) argues that individuals are conscious of their own interests as a result of their perceptions of both themselves and their world. 'They think they know what is in their best interest, even though the process through which their consciousness was formed was influenced to some extent by those who exercise power' (p. 89). This power can be perceived as the power of society, the institution, the department or the discipline. From this basis it is possible to assume that academics perceive scholarship, learning and teaching within the frameworks that guide their everyday lives within the academy, irrespective of whether the basis of their perceptions is correct. In other words academics may have a false perception of their own interests because they have learned nonreflectively to accept what those in authority tell them is in their best interest or in the best interest of the department, institution, etc. The more knowledge academics have about their academic situation, however, the more likely they are to be aware of the 'real' interests. Using this knowledge can help academics to meet the perceived needs of the discipline, department or institution and to establish their academic careers within the power base of their field or institution. Such actions are very prevalent in the established disciplines. The arguments and issues surrounding power within the disciplines are discussed in detail in Chapter 5. What is important here is that the individual's interest and need to learn can, and does, direct what academics perceive to be scholarship and its role within the academic community.

# The purpose of scholarship

Scholarship is a means by which a discipline can adapt to the context in which it is practised. In a time where change is so rapid, does scholarship change as the field changes? What role does scholarship play in making sense of our daily practice as academics? The critical question here is 'Scholarship for what and what purpose should it serve?' (Allen 2002: 3). Senge (2000) suggests that practitioners need to spend 30 per cent of their time reflecting in order to make sense of the world. His perspective on the importance of reflection and understanding the system points us towards an answer to the question 'What is the purpose of scholarship?'

The purpose of scholarship is to provide leadership for the field. This involves fulfilling seven different roles that help practitioners: make meaning of their work; increase their understanding of the whole system; identify key relationships within their disciplines; connect past with present and future; identify what is missing in the present and articulate alternative visions of our future; identify emergent practices and theories; and create connective wisdom in the field.

The discussion on scholarship centres on the relationship between practice and research. Allen (2002) suggests that an assumption is made by practitioners that scholarship needs to change to meet the different demands and contexts of the variety of fields in higher education. This implies that scholarship centres on the relationship between practice and research, and that the question to be framed is: 'Is practice a form of theory or is research an academic pursuit distinct from practice?'

Practice can mean quite contained, individualistic, technical activities. Of course, activities and practices are never merely technical; some content is always implicit. Understanding practice in broader terms is essential in understanding change and how to learn from deliberate attempts to change things. Therefore, it is more helpful to use the term 'practice' in ways that ensure that its substantive content is embraced. MacIntyre (1981) defines practice as:

> any coherent and complex form of socially established co-operative activity through which goods internal to that activity are realised, in the course of trying to achieve those standards of excellence which are appropriate to, and partially definitive of, that form of activity, with the result that human powers to achieve excellence, and human conceptions of the goods and ends involved, are systematically extended. . . . [B]rick-laying is not a

practice; architecture is. Planting turnips is not a practice; farming is. So are the enquiries of physics, chemistry and biology.

(p. 175)

This definition is important when thinking about the purpose of scholarship, as MacIntyre further distinguishes practices from institutions – arguing, for example, that medicine is a practice whereas hospitals are institutions. Similarly, education is a practice, while universities are the institutions established to sustain it. MacIntyre also acknowledges that institutions are necessary to sustain practices, but that institutional politics sometimes distorts or even subverts their purposes:

> For no practice can survive any length of time unsustained by institutions. . . . [I]nstitutions and practices characteristically form a single causal order in which the ideals and creativity of the practice are always vulnerable to the acquisitiveness of the institution, in which the co-operative care for common goods of the practice is always vulnerable to the competitiveness of the institution.
>
> (p. 181)

MacIntyre's insights into the meaning of practice and the relationship it has to institutions help shed light on why the purpose of scholarship becomes entangled between research, theory and practice. However, although the idea of institutions interpreting and reinterpreting practice is important, the main focus here is on practice. Yet practice does have significant associations with institutional behaviours, norms and expectations. These can be considered through Bourdieu's 'theory of practice', in that for Bourdieu practice refers to the ongoing mix of human activities that make up the richness of everyday social life (in this case, the everyday life of the university). For Bourdieu, practices arise from the operation of 'habitus', where habitus is the mediating link between objective social structures and individual action and refers to the embodiment in individual actors of systems of social norms, understandings and patterns of behaviours, which, while not wholly determining action, do ensure that individuals are disposed to act in some ways rather than others. Thompson (1991) suggests that habitus is a set of dispositions that incline agents to act and react in certain ways. The dispositions generate practices, perceptions and attitudes which are regular without being consciously co-ordinated or governed by any rule. This gives some indication as to why and how academics position themselves in the practices of academic life. The purpose of scholarship for academics must therefore lie within the practices of academic activity.

Jarvis (1998) suggests that information about practice exists in two quite distinct forms. The first is the integrated knowledge of practice, which stems from research into practice, e.g. nursing knowledge; the second stems from the discipline, either as unitary or multidisciplinary knowledge about practice (p. 144). Jarvis's categorization of theory and practice offers four formulations, two of which are pertinent to the discussion on the purpose of scholarship; these are theory about practice and theory of and about practice.

Theory about practice is an interesting concept which may help to position the purpose of research. Within the formulation of theory about practice two key elements exist. First, there is knowledge for practice, learned by studying the academic disciplines that underlie practice. For example, it is important for a doctor to have knowledge about anatomy, a policeman to know about the law. Then there is the knowledge about the profession or occupation based on the academic discipline such as sociology, philosophy and economics. The latter makes no pretence of being applicable to practice, but tends to contextualize it (Jarvis 1998: 146).

Within this context the learning is cognitive, but may be useful to practice in a general or holistic way. It is the type of knowledge that can help formulate policy about a discipline or a profession. It is this aspect of theory about practice that could be conceptualized as research, as the knowledge gained does not always have a direct bearing on what practice is. However, Jarvis argues that practitioners whose priority is immediate relevancy will be primarily interested in content knowledge, but this does not mean that the knowledge about practice should not be available to them or that they should not be given other intellectual tools to understand metatheoretical formulations about their work (p. 146). Is this not then the purpose of scholarship?

The second of Jarvis's formulations refers to theory of and about practice, which constitutes the knowledge gained as a result of learning in the cognitive domain. It is not tested in practice, so in a sense it remains 'merely academic'. Its legitimacy lies in the authority of the source of the information, in the internal logic of the information (p. 147). This type of knowledge may well equate to research. Maybe it is for this reason that academic teaching has a strong orientation towards theory. Courses for example are promoted in the mathematical foundations of neo-classical economics and in the methodology of the social sciences. In most disciplines, the theoretical basis of the discipline is central to the structure of the curriculum. Furthermore, the teaching of theory – and indeed the teaching process itself – is commonly separated from practice (Martin 1998).

The status and power of the academic profession are linked to autonomy from influential groups. Theoretical knowledge is the preserve of the academic, and hence has significant prestige. It also helps to sustain the ideology of value-free knowledge. Equally important is the view that academics are under continual pressure to integrate theory and practice in teaching. This is particularly the case in professions such as medicine and dentistry. The pressure to integrate theory based on research and practice has two dominant motivations. One is the advantage of tying knowledge to particular applications and particular interest groups. The other is the realization that learning is usually much more effective when theory and practice are linked (Jarvis 1998: 87). The consequence is the recurring struggle between pressures, particularly those linked to academic self-interest and making courses more theoretical, and those linked to outside interests or social goals that are used to structure learning around a combination of theory and practice.

## Scholarship and scholars

No question is more central to the identity of a scholar than the question of what counts as scholarship. Parks (1997) suggests that the boundaries around the scholarly enterprise must be drawn generously. The meaning of scholarship evaporates if we are unwilling to entertain that some things are not scholarship, and if we were to draw a line, where would that line be? This requires us to consider what the minimal requirements are for something to count as scholarship. What will the scholar accept or reject? Parks argues that there must be a counterbalance between the proliferations of scholarly forms even if the boundaries between disciplines are merging and often fading. Contrast this with Lyotard's (1984) view, that the knowledge game is a social process whereby discourses develop to segregate legitimate and nonlegitimate frameworks for action. Lyotard (1988) argues that within any discipline there are likely to be a variety of such discourses, displaying conflicts between the expressed languages of the discourse even though the content may seem very similar. These differences are a critical way of strengthening alternative views, but they can create problems in reconciling the surface difference against the deeper consensus of beliefs and meanings. These two perspectives raise questions as to the legitimacy of scholarship and the role and function it has to play within the academic community.

Scholars are expected to be concerned with the development of knowledge that is generalizable (i.e. knowledge which is in principle acontextual and ahistorical). Scholars are primarily concerned with developing knowledge that can be defined as 'true knowledge'. Scholarly research needs to be able to justify the validity of accepted approaches to data collection and analysis. Validity is really a word for the standardization of quality across a particular interest group; it is a key sign in the legitimating of knowledge practice. It is interesting to note here that Coleridge's view was that the sole practicable employment for the human mind was to observe, to collect and to classify. However, when talking about literary works, Parks (1997) suggests that scholarship deals not so much with direct emotional experiences as with our attempts to reflect upon and understand them. Scholarly value cannot be attributed to work simply because its personal narrative evokes powerful emotional responses. Parks further argues that most forms of scholarship develop traditions and procedures that simultaneously acknowledge and guard against such motives. To make his point he cites an old Hebrew saying: 'Out of the envy of scholars, wisdom grows.'

## Scholarship and the ideals of education

The definition and appraisal of scholarship is not unrelated to the importance of ideals in education. The term 'scholarship' reflects a philosophical outlook more than it does educational research, the psychology of learning or traditional conceptions of scholarly enquiry. Fincher (2000) suggests that the origin of scholarship, as most scholars understand it, is implicit in the freedom of scholars to pursue their intellectual interest, to read and to write and to discuss their findings and conclusions with others of similar intellect and temperament. Evans (2002), on the other hand, argues that the scholar's task is to frame or identify questions and that the questions do not necessarily have to be invented by the researcher. The primary task is to recognize that the questions exist, and have bearing on the subject in hand, the emphasis being not only on asking or answering the questions, but on the very nature of the academic enquiry taking place.

The ideal of questioning, intellectual pursuit and the awakening of the mind to the need for criticism is key to the Socratic approach to education and scholarship. 'The Socratic education begins . . . with the awakening of the mind to the need for criticism, to the uncertainty of principles by which it supposed itself to be guided' (Anderson 1980: 69). Criticism here seeks to show that wisdom is not thinking that you know what you don't know. Socrates is wise to the extent that he does not claim to have knowledge by a ruthless examination of the claims of individuals to have knowledge or wisdom. The Socratic approach is not an empirical method proceeding by reference to facts, but a rationalist approach that works through the exposure of con-tradictions in a person's thinking. For Socrates, there is no end to the process of critical questioning, and education is solely about learning to be critical.

The fundamental principle of education is clearly expressed in Plato's *Republic*. Socrates describes the parable of the cave, how men rise from the darkness of the world of phenomena and uncertainties of belief into the radiant land of knowledge:

> Education is not what some people declare it to be. They say that they put into the soul knowledge that was not there before, like putting sight into blind eyes. . . .
>
> And the art of education is then concerned with this very question: how man shall most easily and completely be turned around. It is not a matter of giving him sight. He possesses that. But he is facing the wrong direction and does not look where he ought. That is the problem.
>
> (quoted in Grube 1935: 234)

The exercise of learning is a Socratic adventure, older than the *paideia* of classical culture or the curriculum of the originating schools of the Platonic Academy and Aristotelian Lyceum in the fourth century BC. In this journey there are many detours and dead-ends as well as arrivals and achievements. The scholarship of the *schola* is taken up into the academic's life; it is the perspective through which he or she can look at life in the world – in circles of understanding and cycles of life. The point here is that it is too late to back away from the concept of scholarship; it is embedded in academic life. Scholarship is a part of how academics think, act and live their lives in the world of academia. With learning as with life, all are engaged; it is only a question of how well. It requires commitment, concentration and imaginative engage-ment to complete the circle of understanding. Scholarship at best is not a response to external directives; it is in and about ourselves as academics.

The Socrates depicted in traditional scholarship seems not only confident that he can discover truth for himself, but also eager to persuade others of that truth – by clever and devious means if necessary.

The importance of the Socratic philosophy rests with the fact that it provides a nonrational or emotional background to his intensive search for understanding in a world overcast by ignorance. As the *Meno* and *Protagoras* indicated, he remained doubtful whether virtue (*arete*) could be taught in the sense of a body of imparted knowledge or an intellectual technique. Yet teaching was important to him and virtue an important subject of enquiry. Socrates is sometimes regarded as having not so much a philosophy as a method, or an attitude to certain problems. He had a technique of asking questions and this technique (*dialektike*) could be used to establish by refutation (*elenchos*) that an apparent expert was ignorant, and could also lead to the point where Socrates and other participants in a discussion became aware of their own ignorance. This characteristic approach employed by Socrates suggests that it is better to establish one's own ignorance cleverly than remain under the illusion that knowledge is truly grasped. Rankin (1983) states:

> This is not a philosophy in the sense of a set of defensible ideas about the nature of god and the universe, the problem of being, the problem of knowing, the moral duties of man, but by implication and allusion it touches upon all human experience and takes cognisance of these areas of investigation. His greatest teaching is his method of teaching, and that is by asking questions. Questions imply answers even when the answers are admissions of ignorance. Questions imply that there is something worth asking about.
>
> (p. 151)

Scholarship is more than calling; it is a matter of excellence of character (*ethos*). That is, there are virtues (from the Greek *arete*) tied to scholarship. The first of these virtues for me is courage, which for Socrates was an essential element of character. Within the academic world, what might this mean? Courage is not always about stepping out into the breach; it can be simply about summoning up the necessary confidence to affirm one's own views and principles in a teaching session or in a publication.

Aristotle (384–322 BC) devotes a good deal of attention to the intellectual virtues, which he characterizes as states of the soul. They are five in number: art, scientific knowledge, practical wisdom, philosophic wisdom and intuitive reason. The central function of these intellectual virtues is to provide methods for knowing what is true and thus to provide the intellectual basis for the selection of the right rule. The importance of both the moral and the intellectual virtues is emphasized in the following passage:

> The origin of action – its efficient, not its final cause – is choice, and that of choice is desire and reasoning with a view to an end. This is why choice cannot exist, either without reason and intellect, or without a moral state; for good action and its opposite cannot exist without a combination of intellect and character. Intellect itself, however, moves nothing but only the intellect, which aims at an end.
>
> (*Ethics*, Book VI, 1139a31)

From an Aristotelian viewpoint education involves teaching the intellectual and moral virtues necessary for right action. 'Virtue is the perfection of reason. Reason is the source of the first principles of knowledge. Reason deals with the abstract and ideal aspects. Active reason makes the world intelligible' (Aristotle 1996). Intellectual virtue in the main owes both its birth and its growth to teaching, where teaching is the greatest form of understanding. Aristotle goes on to suggest that control of action is equally important to development: 'There are three things in the soul which control action and truth – sensation, reason, desire' (1941: 11139a17). In theories of modern decision-making, sensation corresponds to beliefs about the true state of nature; desire corresponds to the evaluation of consequences, and reason to the choice of the action or decision that maximizes expected value. For Aristotle 'all human beings hunger to know by their very nature'. If this is true, then it can be argued that learning is done naturally for the love of knowing and understanding and not for its utility. Learning is an end, not a means to something else. For Aristotle; education and teaching are always about an object and should have content. 'Education is preparation for some worthy activity' (Davidson 1900: 169). In the Aristotelian teaching act, the teacher instructs a learner about some object, some body of knowledge or some discipline. 'Teaching and learning never represent merely an interpersonal relationship or the expression of feelings. They are always about disciplined inquiry into some aspect of reality . . .

developing and cultivating each person's rationality' (Ornstein & Levine 1981: 112–13).

From the philosophical aspirations of Socrates, Plato and Aristotle, it is possible to begin to understand how the ideal of education focuses on learning and rationality, elements which clearly distinguish activity in university from school. Universities cannot function without the element of learning, the nature of which combines learning on the collective and individual levels – that is, it comprises both research and studying, or at least it is an interface between the two, by making knowledge developed by the few available to the many (Rothblatt 1997). Communication of learning outcomes and activities that take place within the university is essential in furthering scholarship. As the Danish philosopher Søren Kierkegaard remarked, 'the secret to communication is to set the other free' (1940). What he had in mind here was an understanding about truth, possibly that 'You shall know the truth and the truth will set you free' (Kierkegaard 1940). This can be interpreted as legal freedom as in liberty, political freedom as in speech and assembly, and academic freedom as in critical expression and imagination. Socrates persuasively argues a necessary correlation between freedom and responsibility. Much later Kant takes up the argument by suggesting 'the grammatical imperative that there is only freedom under law' (2002). So too with imagination: freedom becomes meaningful, becomes an art, only under the formal discipline of commitment. This philosophical approach to understanding scholarship is an essential part of an academic's life. Socrates described the basic task of philosophy as trying to understand what it is we already know. Here lies a fundamental question for professors: as a professor, what is it exactly that you profess? How and to whom do you profess it? It is interesting to consider Leo Tolstoy's views of understanding what it is we already know. In his *Confessions*, reflecting on his life and work as a famous novelist, and reflecting on the value of what he was doing, he wrote that the single justification of his life and profession was as a (moral) teacher. The importance of this synthesis of thought to the academic community is significant. How many academics find with some discomfort that they have nothing to profess, an absence of creative passion or sustaining principles, and too little commitment to higher education's principles and values? Why has it come to the point where academics can and do feel they no longer have anything to profess? Have the ideals of higher education eluded the academic community or do we need alternative means of understanding how these ideals are constructed, interpreted and implemented?

Kierkegaard's central problematic, which was *how to become a Christian in Christendom*, is a useful philosophical quandary in helping us to consider and understand why some academics flounder in the present academic environment, particularly when such fundamental concepts as scholarship no longer appear to have a generic meaning or common understanding. If the problematic is reconstructed to say 'how to become an academic within academia', then Kierkegaard's synthesis could be argued as follows. The task is most difficult for the well educated, since prevailing educational and cultural institutions tend to produce stereotyped members of the 'crowd' (university), rather than to allow individuals to discover their own unique identities. Placing this problematic in the context of the social and cultural environments of higher education is fascinating. Currently academics, particularly in the UK, have to research, teach, and be involved in administration, and those in the USA strive for tenure. This forces a stereotyping of requirements on academics, often not allowing them to become who they are beyond the boundaries of their socially imposed identities. This is a particularly significant point, when staff across the sector are asking questions about the status of academics, especially whether they are teachers with teaching-only contracts or researchers with research-only contracts or a combination of both. These pressures create tensions around their identities, sense of belonging, needs and interests, and their consequent engagement with academic activities.

## Scholarship in conflict

There are many structural problems within higher education that impinge on the quality of scholarship and teaching and on the drive towards academic reform. These problems are reflected in recent debates and conflicts surrounding the reward incentives and structures that set the priorities for academic work and the methods of measuring academic success. Sometimes academics' personal measures of success fail to match the institutional measures by which institutions reward their performance (Oakley 1995; Hahn 1990). Moreover, the rhetoric of many institutions often fails to match the real indicators of recognition by which academic advancement – or even survival – is assured. Academics are no different from other humans; they respond to genuine and authentic criteria of promotion and advancement, whether or not these criteria actually match institutional rhetoric.

Within the UK the promotion of academics and the Research Assessment Exercise drive academic endeavour and scholarly production. In the USA it is the 'tyranny of academic tenure', perceived as academe's sacred initiation rite and as a treasured professional growth experience (LeBaron 2001). Academic tenure is the bedrock of academic careerism, which, according to Chait (1997a, 1997b), requires thoughtful reconsideration free from the ideological blinkers of its most fervent advocates and opponents. Although the notion of tenure no longer exists in the UK, promotion through research activity that is identified as scholarly activity, and scholarship, still remains the basis for promotion to the rank of professor. Perley (1997) suggests that some of the formal associations of professor, however, defend the traditional structures of academic tenure with a fervour that occasionally crosses the boundary separating scholarly discourse from passionate antagonism.

According to its apologists, tenure assures the academic autonomy that promotes independent thinking and free expression. In reality it often does precisely the opposite (Smith 1990). Academics who do not have tenure or do not achieve promotion continue to work under the prevailing attitudes imposed by the cultural values of the established professors or tenured staff, who typically in turn reflect and endorse departmental and institutional orthodoxies. LeBaron (2001) argues that academic autonomy, so prized by the defenders of academic promotion through research and scholarship in the UK, and tenure in the USA, produces academic isolation, tending to separate professors not only from administrators but also from one another across departments. This impedes meaningful dialogue about scholarship, and especially teaching. Higher education is alone among professions to sequester the substance of its primary function – scholarship – from administrative participation. In almost any other type of enterprise, this would be considered nothing short of madness (LeBaron 2001: 4). Winston (1994) takes this argument further by stating that he deplores the increasingly dominant tendency of universities to concentrate their professorial recruitment on 'superstar' research faculty, affording them privileges and remuneration packages that reduce 'the value of teaching in the faculty market' (p. 42). The result of such actions, according to Winston, is workplace resentment of the generous discretionary (that is, non-courseload) time given to the superstars resulting in their lower-paid colleagues not only carrying a disproportionate teaching load, but also being denied equitable time to pursue their own scholarly projects (p. 44).

The culture of rewarding and sustaining scholarly output through research at the expense of teaching causes significant conflict within the higher-education community. It also discourages risk-taking because real career rewards (such as promotion and increased salary) are keyed to the most conservative behaviours. The orthodoxies of academic departments discourage cross-disciplinary research, teaching or scholarship, despite the common knowledge that real life is not compartmentalized by disciplines.

Debates over academic priorities and the ideals of scholarship within the community – about publishing or perishing, about teaching versus research, about interest versus need – are now being extended beyond the academic arena of promotion and tenure, and have become a key area for political interference, particularly in the UK with the publication of the Higher Education Bill (2004). Within the USA it is also clear that an increasing value is attached to teaching and that this is being championed through the mantra 'the scholarship of teaching'. This in itself has created further conflict, due to a lack of understanding about what the scholarship of teaching might mean and the nature of engagement it might require in order for it to be recognized and rewarded.

There have been endless reports and research papers indicating a strong sense of conflict between teaching and research imperatives. Those committed to teaching find themselves torn between their concerns for supplying high-quality teaching in the classroom, and the demands of grant-writing and project management of research and publication that are viewed as essential for professional advancement both within their institutions and within their chosen disciplines. As early as 1987 Boyer reported that academic staff felt a considerable tension in relation to the divide between professional loyalties and competing career concerns, explicitly the tension between scholarship and teaching (Boyer 1987: 6).

Lucas (1996) has indicated that the unrest and conflict lie in the fact that most academics are sceptical about prospects for changing an academic ethos that was begun more than a century ago in America and even longer ago in Europe. Lucas cites Johns Hopkins University as the propagator of the research university following the German research university model, which has subsequently been adopted widely across America. This has generated arguments such as those put forward by Barnett (1992), who states that 'despite declarations that teaching and research are inescapably incompatible, reforming the academic culture means challenging deeply ingrained notions of institutional prestige and status. When universities raid one another's faculties, it has been said, they do not do it because they seek cutting-edge classroom teachers' (p. 40). Lucas (1996) goes on to argue that the continuous tensions felt by academics have an inevitable outcome – that of a 'failure to discriminate between quality and quantity – which leads to an ever-increasing accumulation of "gun-point scholarship"' (p. 191). This of course is borne out by the continued conversations that are not about quality, but simply about research 'output' and 'scholarly production'.

Against this historical background it is surprising that, relatively speaking, so few academics question or challenge a system that tends to denigrate teaching and to overemphasize scholarly publication as the basis of academic reward. As Lucas suggests, 'at one level, part of the answer probably lies in the reluctance of the individual academic to question a system in which they have acquired a vested interest' (p. 195). As is discussed in detail in Chapter 5, this issue becomes a mainstay for those involved in scholarly activities within a discipline-based culture.

> To criticise established norms, to wonder openly about the propriety of a system that insists that each new initiate demonstrates scholarly prowess in a public forum, to subject research and scholarship to peer review is to risk being branded irresponsible, threatened, or incompetent. Fear of ridicule and failure is often a powerful reinforcer working to keep people in line.
>
> (Lucas 1996: 196)

Historically it is quite plain to see that the sheer pressure of the systematic imperative to research, publish and create scholarly works has made it easy to ignore other equally important aspects of academic life such as teaching and learning. 'Again historically this has been a lost opportunity, as it appears it has been the student who has paid the price for the commonplace neglect of teaching as an intellectual challenge and object of reflection in its own right' (Diamond 1994: 20).

## Scholarship's next move?

Globally there has been an increased interest in the role of teaching and learning in higher education. Focal points of research have been in America, Australia and the United Kingdom. Each has taken its own perspectives on what the new initiatives and interest may be, or may constitute, from the major input of the Carnegie Foundation in the USA to the Higher Education Academy in the UK. But what is clear is that teaching and learning, and the role scholarship may play within teaching and learning, have become the subject of both academic enquiry and political interest. As Donald Kennedy of Stanford University so eloquently stated, 'it is time for us to reaffirm that education – that is teaching in all forms – is the primary task of higher education and should be commended' (quoted in Boyer 1990: 1). Such a statement is brave but necessary, but it also needs to be accepted that to act on this reaffirmation is to pose a full challenge to the dominant aspects, and professional norms, of the higher-education community. Only history will judge its success or failure, but what is essential is a need to reconceptualize scholarship.

*Part 2*

# Policy and power: influences on scholarship

## Chapter 3

# Policy and initiatives: the need to reconceptualize scholarship

*Simon Lygo-Baker*

> If I have exhausted the justifications I have reached the bedrock and my spade is turned. Then I am inclined to say 'This is simply what I do'.
>
> (Wittgenstein)

Chapter 2 has introduced and discussed what scholarship might be and the activities that scholars may engage in to produce scholarly work and scholarship. It has also suggested that being a member of the academy is equivalent to being immersed in the world of scholarship. Yet increasingly the world of scholarship and the higher-education community are being influenced and pressurized from external agencies, particularly government in the case of the UK and Australia. One of the most significant areas of policy development and intrusion has been in teaching and learning. This has produced an increased focus on the scholarly approaches taken to teaching and learning, as well as the scholarly products of the learning activities through scholarship.

In principle there is no reason why policy documents and higher-education initiatives aimed at enhancing teaching and learning should not make reference to the concept of scholarship. The difficulty is that although 'scholarship' is generally understood as a word relating to the work of those in higher education, defining what scholarship currently means causes more than a little difficulty. The original associations of the term have contracted so that scholarship has become equated almost solely with research and any attempt to broaden the definition leads to confusion and dispute. As was discussed in Chapter 2, an outcome of this contraction has been for the processes that relate to the end product of scholarship to become the defining aspects of the general term. In other words scholarship is defined as peer-reviewed papers and research findings. When Boyer (1990) wrote *Scholarship Reconsidered* he invited the academic community to reflect on the concept of scholarship and how it is interpreted within the academy. His definition reminded us of the place that teaching has within academia and that this was and should be seen as part of a conceptualization of scholarship. Such reconsideration and highlighting of the role of scholarship was timely, and has helped to raise debates within the academy as to the depth and breadth of the meaning of scholarship and its related activities. Boyer's original work came at a time when the concept of scholarship, and in particular the scholarship of teaching, was increasingly being adopted within policy statements and documents relating to the enhancement of teaching and learning in higher education.

Confusion has arisen, however, as a result of ambiguity over the meaning of scholarship and this has resulted in a lack of clarity in the related terms, such as 'the scholarship of teaching'. For the term 'scholarship' to assist our knowledge and understanding, the definition needs to be clear and understood *in* context but not *because of* the context. Once the conceptualization of scholarship is clear then the intended understanding of related terms becomes clearer and can help describe associated phenomena. For example, when someone states that they are 'going to ride a bicycle' there is general understanding of the meaning of 'bicycle'. Related terms can then be applied to this meaning to explain the production of a bicycle, how to ride a bicycle, and so on, and these add to the understanding of the general term 'bicycle'. The understanding of these related terms becomes confused and ambiguous without the meaning allied to the general term being understood.

Through the drawing together of the historical and philosophical arguments relating to scholarship, a view is gained of the context and environment in which policy documents and higher-education initiatives are driving the academy, in the name of improving teaching and learning. Such a synthesis allows us to begin to understand whether this policy drive is one drawn from a sound conceptualization of scholarship or one drawn from a particular conceptualization and context that facilitates and propagates the stated policies or initiatives.

Currently policies and initiatives, particularly in the UK, appear to be congested with ideas and issues relating to excellent teaching, expert knowledge and methods aimed at evaluating and measuring what constitutes effective teaching and research. Such drives and initiatives should act as a warning to the academy. It is time for the academy to reawaken, rediscover and restore what it understands by scholarship as a concept, so that its voice is heard and can make an impact within the ongoing debates from the perspective of 'learners'. Unless the academy forcefully engages in the debate, alternative interpretations of scholarship may continue to be created, accepted and utilized not by 'learners' but by policy makers (see Figure 3.1). Evidence to date (Shulman 1998) suggests that the current debate surrounding the meaning associated with the notion of the scholarship of teaching is limiting the definition. For the scholarship of teaching to be accepted as having value and meaning within and to society the definition needs to be clear so that it assists our understanding of the broader term 'scholarship'. The danger is that without a clear conceptualization of scholarship there is nothing to ground the scholarship of teaching in, which leads to definitions being narrow, imprecise and related to what they are not, rather than providing an understanding of what they are. The academy needs to respond to the interpretations being consolidated in current policies and reconceptualize scholarship to ensure that any related concepts, such as the scholarship of teaching, are definitions that bring meaning to the context of higher education and not vehicles used to drive through policy.

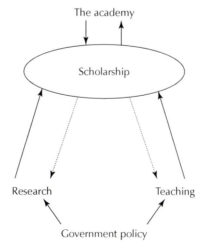

*Figure 3.1* Interpretations of the term 'scholarship'

# Historical and philosophical arguments

In order to understand the implications that the meaning of scholarship might have for current debates it is important to look back at the historical and philosophical development of the concept of scholarship. Contextualizing scholarship facilitates the understanding of possible misinterpretations and perceptions, thus enabling the reconsideration of current perspectives and future visions. The definition of scholarship has changed over time from an initial view that it was related to someone who is able to 'devote himself to the culture of the mind' (De Wulf 1956). This original interpretation encompassed the traditional Greek view of teaching as everybody's task and therefore nobody's in particular. This began to break down when subjects such as mathematics were developed and it became patently obvious that not everybody could actually teach them. The concept of scholarship slowly found itself embedded more closely with the notion of discovery, a narrowing of the original definition and use of the term. John Stuart Mill's notion that humans progress intellectually when freedom of thought and discussion leads to the continuous improvement of ways of doing things sees scholarship as enhancing life by providing understanding and meaning. This role fell to the academic who was a scholar, engaged in scholarship.

As far back as Aristotle the role of scholarship as a broader concept that encompassed teaching was appreciated. Through discovery, Aristotle suggested, an individual might escape towards knowledge and understanding. However, this person retained a moral obligation to provide society with service and not to desert humanity. Discovery needed to be shared, not hoarded by an individual or an elite community. Knowledge too should be shared, and used to provide understanding through education. This definition of scholarship therefore was wide enough to encompass the role of discovery and the utilization of this for the good of society. As time has elapsed the concept appears to have found itself more easily equated with the initial phase of discovery and research and not to encompass teaching. As Whitsitt (1990) suggests, most people outside academia only hear about scholarship when something startling takes place: in other words another discovery. As a result the traditional view of teaching that has emerged sees the key as instruction in the known and delivery of the accepted. Boyer's work can be seen to be an attempt to re-establish teaching within a broader definition by suggesting that the conceptualization of scholarship is only meaningful when it goes beyond the stage of discovery alone.

The work of Boyer, whilst not ground-breaking, has brought back for debate within the academy early conceptions of scholarship which have been revisited regularly in the last fifteen years. Much is owed to Boyer for challenging the narrowness of definitions of scholarship. His suggestion of a four-part conceptual framework, which is discussed further in Chapter 7, encourages a broader boundary, which has been further promoted by Parks (1997). This inevitably brings with it difficulties of definition and as a result the term remains highly contested. For example, Boyer fails to differentiate between excellent teaching and the scholarship of teaching. Whilst at first this may not appear to be particularly important, it seems that this has been exploited by those wishing to define the work of an academic and has created room for misinterpretation. A number of Boyer's colleagues at the Carnegie Institute have attempted to resolve some of these difficulties. For example, Glassick et al. (1997) in *Scholarship Assessed* suggest that the scholarship of teaching is more than excellent teaching; it entails practice that leads to new understanding, something that can be seen, is open and available to others. They argue that scholarship requires current knowledge and with regard to teaching involves exploring student learning. Others, such as Trigwell (2001) and Glassick (1997), have attempted to find criteria by which to classify what scholarly activity is within the teaching and learning environment. A significant problem with these current definitions of scholarship is that they often define scholarly activity as the relationship of action to other things and not simply in terms of what constitutes scholarship.

Although Boyer's work was important there is a danger, as Weimer (Menges and Weimar 1996) states, that 'if notions of a scholarship of teaching are not soon made real and substantive in publications, policies and practices, this nice phrase will be replaced by some trendier term'. The result will be that the conceptualization will remain narrow and, as Wittgenstein warned, people will create a private language that is only understood and spoken within a particular area. Currently the danger is that those outside the academy are creating such a private language. A definition needs to be found that not only provides conventional meaning but enables people to penetrate the depths of reality and to see what it is and what it is not. This requires recognition of the difference between merely naming something and defining it. Providing a name may suggest a general meaning but it does little else. For example, saying 'that object is a table' means nothing until the object is defined. The danger here is that although defining goes beyond merely giving something a name this can still be limited. Something can be defined by exploring what it is in relation to other things, which suggests what it is not. For example, a table can be defined by exploring what makes up a dining table and a set of dining chairs. This tells us that a table has a relationship with a chair and dining, but it does not tell us what a table is. To gain full understanding the 'something' needs to be explored for what it is in itself. Scholarship can be used just as a name but this will afford little meaning and no consensus. It can also be defined in relation to other things or what it really means. The danger of the work of Boyer is that by identifying four different areas of scholarship it creates a temptation to define each stage in terms of what it is *not* in relation to the other three: scholarship is defined relatively rather than for what it is. As a result it becomes important to confine definitions by examining what the peculiar and characteristic elements are that distinguish the various aspects of scholarship as well as the common elements that are a legitimate part of it.

Although Boyer created much of the impetus by raising the profile of scholarship and in particular the scholarship of teaching, his work provided us with very little by way of definition. This has led other writers to take up the challenge. Badley (2003) argues that in breaking down the definition within each aspect Boyer still fails to acknowledge key aspects within each stage. For example, the scholarship of teaching is defined according to the role of the teacher and teaching to the exclusion of students and learning. As teaching and learning are inextricably linked this definition is intrinsically unstable. Trigwell et al. (2000) take this point forward and suggest that scholarly teaching is about making 'transparent how we have made learning possible' (p. 156). This adds an important acknowledgement of the link between teaching and learning. Other writers have taken up the reins and attempted to forge a definition with real meaning (Cross & Steadman 1996, Glassick et al. 1997, Kreber 2001). Within many of these there are some key themes that recur: scholarship is about engagement; reflection; communication and dissemination. Trigwell et al. add a fourth dimension: conceptualizing teaching and learning. Within their work this equates to being informed about the theory and literature, relating this to the discipline, and being able to collect and present evidence to prove effectiveness as a teacher. Such consideration shows that definitions which equate excellent teaching and the scholarship of teaching are misguided. Teaching may be excellent and viewed as such by peers and learners without excellent teachers engaging in any reflection or conceptualizing their teaching and learning.

Other attempts to move the debate further have looked at developing a more process-driven model. Glassick (1997) notes that all the forms of scholarship that Boyer identified have a series of common unfolding stages. He suggests that when work of whatever type is praised in terms of scholarship it is done according to the following qualitative standards: clear goals; adequate preparation; appropriate methods; significant results; effective communication and reflective critique. This suggests that such a process can be identified within all forms of scholarship and may appear at first glance to be an attractive solution to the debates that have taken place. If scholarship can be defined as a process that is universal whatever the element being described, then it can be more easily recognized. In contrast to this Rice (1992) argues that scholarship cannot merely be described as a process to be ticked off at various points: it is a far more complex, integrated and interrelated phenomenon. He suggests that when scholarship is defined in relation to teaching it must show these crucial elements: the ability to draw complex strands together to produce meaning and to place it in context; the ability to forge the divide between intellectual substance and the teaching process; and finally understanding how students develop meaning from the teaching received. Ironically perhaps, Rice himself is criticized for oversimplification by Badley, who argues that once again the last strand is far too simplistic a definition of the complex relationship that exists between the teacher and the learner.

Hutchings and Shulman (1999) echo the need for scholarship to be seen as something that is transparent, that can be recognized and regarded by others in all of its forms. Academics will doubtless associate this with their role as discoverer, interpreter and researcher, but is this the case with regard to the area that Aristotle identified as their moral obligation to assist others with understanding by teaching? Shulman is clear that scholarship involves the academic community in engagement through communication, evaluating ideas and critiquing these through peer review. In research this is recognized and accepted. In teaching, however, it is far more contested. Indeed, it is a far from simple process for, as he suggests, certain variables need to be considered. These include the discipline that people work within, the students and their learning, the context that learning occurs in and the academics' own identity. This suggests scholarship involves the convergence of an individual's disciplinary, moral, communal and personal motives; it is not something that can be achieved or considered in isolation. On the one hand, scholarship is about the integrity of the individual and how they view being scholarly, and on the other it is about how and where this person fits within the context of their teaching and learning environment. This suggests that there needs to be a convergence and reconciliation of the values of the individual and those of the discipline within which they work. Indeed, as Sullivan (2003) argues:

> The primary 'tools' of the scholar are neither the sources (or media) through which s/he works, nor the method s/he employs in interrogating these. While the nature of the material one studies and the reliability of the methods one uses are crucial, what determines the effectiveness of scholarship are the 'inner tools', the personal qualities, moral and spiritual, of the scholar.
>
> (p. 127)

This may provide the clue to one of the difficulties of relating scholarship to teaching. Teaching has been seen, and often remains seen, as something isolated and insular: an activity undertaken alone. Shulman suggests that the results of the learning process need to be more open so that the integrity and the values of the teacher become exposed. This exposure needs to go beyond the discipline to encompass the notion of scholarship as it relates to academia. The result is that the values of the individual need to find expression within the discipline and to be accepted, while the disciplinary values need to be recognized within the overall values that define scholarship. For although values can be recognized as having been drawn from the discipline and the individual scholar, if scholarship exists beyond being a calling then it is bounded within a series of shared values as well. And yet, what are these values? How are they defined?

## The importance of values in understanding and defining scholarship

Values are 'the determiners in man that influence his choices in life and that thus decide his behaviour' (Inlow 1972). An individual's values are developed from both unique individual experiences and from their 'social' identity (Breakwell 1986 and Inlow 1972). Sullivan (2003) suggests that these values are expressed through the 'habits of recognition' that result from each person's *habitus*. The pattern is developed from a cumulative series of experiences and decisions made over time that shape our future responses. These values, according to Craft (2000), shift depending upon the setting within which people find themselves and as such are open to the influence of professional or 'collective' values. According to McInnis (1993), although there are differences between different academic disciplines there are some 'strongly shared values amongst academics'. A number of writers, such as Becher (2001), have examined the notion of the existence of an academic identity drawn from common values. This suggests that an understanding of scholarship can be drawn from those engaged in value trading and development within academic roles and not from those attempting to define it from outside, such as policy writers.

Understanding what these shared values may be is fraught with difficulty, as Badley (2003) points out. The different disciplines will continue to bring different interpretations to the table, because each discipline has its own history and background which influences what, where, when, how and why things are taught and learned. Each has a traditional set of pedagogical expressions to enable these factors to be translated, and anyone who has worked across disciplines will have noted the similarities and disparities between them. Huber and Morreale (2002) argue that knowledge of teaching and learning is inevitably going to be drawn from the discipline of each person and that this may empower individuals to investigate and understand teaching and learning within their own corner of expression and interest. However, they point out that whilst drawing these from the discipline can be useful in providing impetus and a context within which to examine teaching and learning, it can also be somewhat restrictive and can limit and question the legitimacy of a term as broad as 'scholarship'. Scholarly effort is not made up of isolated decisions but develops from an accumulation of experiences and activities carried out by multidimensional individuals interacting with others and within a range of social habitats. Each individual brings his or her own observation, critique and reflection to the scholarly endeavour and this makes speaking a language that all recognize, understand and then respond to extremely difficult. As a result the notion of scholarship in relation to teaching and learning may appear to sit uncomfortably within the higher-education arena. But is this only a perceived problem or one that has substance?

It is essential here to question whether or not disciplines are mutually exclusive. It is possible to identify common ground between the disciplines and to argue that scholarship can be seen as the conceptual base upon which the interpretation and understanding of the role of the academic within a discipline can be regulated and understood. This view is not without critics – the Carnegie Foundation for example suggests that within the scholarship of teaching, 'learning is deeply embedded in the discipline; its questions arise from the character of the field and what it means to know it deeply'. But do the questions come out of the field to the exclusion of all other disciplines? If so then perhaps there is no common conception of scholarship, only individual disciplines' separate conceptions of scholarship in relation to teaching and learning. This again raises questions about the academic community and academic identities. The Carnegie scholars are right to suggest that the scholarship of teaching is about practice but they need to consider that the reason it is so hard to distinguish from the actual practice of teaching is because the practical element is embedded within the scholarship of teaching, not something that emerges only from the practice. In other words scholarship exists as a concept before, during and after the actual practice of teaching. To incorporate the element of teaching within the concept there is a need to consider what goes on before teaching, during teaching and during the reflection that occurs afterwards. It is also important to take account of the element of learning throughout this. For true scholarship to occur, it is the engagement of this learning that is the key. This takes the concept beyond the provision of scholarly work or the practice of teaching and engages with the scholarship of teaching (Richlin 2001). This relates to developing knowledge by means of learning, including learning by the academic about how to engage learners. Scholarship begins where learning begins.

## Policy

Birch (1988) has suggested that academics have become so preoccupied with investigating the source of theories that for the most part they have ignored what it is for someone to actually know how to perform a task. The danger is that scholarship is seen as something that helps to explain the world that exists and therefore how people should behave within it. This leads to the development of general statements and excessive attention to the implications of these, which can, Birch argues, lead to serious gaps in our understanding. In regard to scholarship this can be seen as having been translated within policy development and is reflected in attempts to define what constitutes good teaching by examining end results without understanding how they have been achieved. The concept of the scholarship of teaching becomes associated with general statements relating to indicators or criteria of good teaching rather than engaging with the serious question of why and how learning did or did not occur. There is very little opportunity to gain understanding because very little conceptual knowledge is considered and very limited investigation is undertaken of how scholarship can be recognized within the work and life of the modern academic.

The result of the increased scrutiny of university standards has led Blake et al. (1998) to suggest that the emphasis comes from the promotion of 'procedural values' over the more important 'content'. Norris (in Elliott 1993) and Medley (in Katz and Raths 1984) do not see such a trend as new. Both argue that attempts to provide indicators relating to the work of academics can be traced back through the twentieth century. The temptation has been to try to offset the 'growing complexity of the academic environment' (Bamber 2002) by producing a simple and unambiguous measure of the aims, purposes and values of higher education. Such a reductionist agenda, however appealing, is unlikely to be able to capture the essence of the role and therefore the conceptual aspects of scholarship.

To be able to conceptualize scholarship, therefore, using teaching as the example, there is a need to understand what it is and how it works. The first factor does not involve proving that someone is a high-quality teacher; it means being able to describe what scholarship looks like, what its features are irrespective of the discipline or a particular issue, and is thus a multidimensional approach. The second factor is about defining what happens in practice and is one-dimensional. It is the latter approach which has attracted the focus of policy makers.

Defining a process – what happens in practice – has become a standard method in the modern era of defining scholarship. The result is a narrowing of the meaning and a suggestion that scholarship can be quantified and is measurable. If we consider the context within which this has occurred, the motivation towards this more simplistic conceptualization becomes more apparent. As Barnett (2000) points out, the postmodern era is one in which frameworks are constantly being contested. It appeals to the policy makers to define the scholarship of teaching in terms of practice because this can be quantified; it appeals to managers because they can manage by it; and it appeals to those who do not wish to conceptualize their teaching because they can follow a process without engaging and attempting to understand. As the complexity of higher education and the society within which it exists grows, the urge to be able to predict action, to understand the individuals within the system, perhaps inevitably also grows (Harre 1998). The antidote is to set criteria or standards which suggest that action or human endeavour can be easily interpreted, understood and, most importantly, measured.

Certainly scholarship as a concept has increasingly found its way into policy documentation without a clear definition that takes account of the multidimensional nature of the concept. Policy-driven definitions treat scholarship as being something that can be measured and reduced to criteria. One example comes from the UK Research Assessment Exercise in which scholarship is 'defined as the creation, development and maintenance of the intellectual infrastructure of subjects and disciplines, in forms such as dictionaries, scholarly editions, catalogues and contributions to major research databases' (RAE 2/99 para 1.12). In other words it can be defined and quantified. It is one-dimensional and Badley points to other Higher Education Funding Council for England (HEFCE) documents as further evidence of this approach.

This adds to the constricted and misleading meaning of the concept of scholarship. Not only is the concept here synonymous with research alone but the interpretation of this is driven by the policy that sets research against criteria that are designed to be measured. If this argument is followed through logically then research becomes exclusively policy driven, with an increase in evidenced-based research that is not necessarily intended to yield new knowledge and understanding – and yet, as we saw in the previous chapter, that was once exactly the role that a scholar was expected to fulfil. Humes and Bryce (2001: 330) argue that the role of the scholar has to take account of the shifts that have occurred and thus contribute in the 'public arena where evidence, knowledge and values constitute contested terrain'. The danger is that the scholar is no longer providing the definition and that this and the context within which it is being reinterpreted are externally driven. The result is that research becomes bounded, the art of discovery and innovation becomes restricted and the conceptualization of scholarship becomes narrower. The dangers do not stop there. The notion and integrity of teaching is no longer allied with scholarship and also becomes controlled by policy makers who create criteria relating to their own standards. These are developed in such a way that the scholarship element of teaching is no longer debated but instead the quality becomes defined by process alone, which is derived from and driven by policy. The meaning, the very essence of scholarship, is reduced to a simple one that can be measured by a set of universal, externally driven criteria.

Scholarship as a concept initially suggested freedom and the opportunity to extend the scope and influence of ideas. The policy agenda in the postmodern era, however, suggests the control and restriction of these. The values of each come into conflict. This then obscures the debate over what actually constitutes scholarship, which becomes lost in a plethora of criteria and documents.

## Reconsideration of the concept

What is required is to strip back our definitions and explore where the confusion begins. Elton (1992) argues that to be scholarly requires an academic to utilize in his or her teaching the same thought processes that he or she applies in his or her research. That does not require the scholarship of teaching to be the same as the scholarship of research. It is the processes which define being scholarly that are the same. This again highlights an important difference between being scholarly and scholarship. One is a process, the other a concept. For example, consider the concept of 'driving'. The processes of driving a bicycle and of driving a car share many overlapping actions but they are not the same. Understanding the process involved in driving as relating to one or the other is different from understanding the concept of driving that relates to both.

Unfortunately the ongoing debate in higher education over the relevant merits of research over teaching often clouds the issue. If the scholarship of teaching involves some aspect of research into teaching and knowing about teaching, then it may not be at odds with the notion that research and teaching are elements within scholarship as a concept. A difficulty that many writers have come up against is a belief that 'Scholarship is manifest in publication, not in the classroom. Little attention seems to be directed toward teaching as an intellectually rigorous activity' (Boys 1999: 129). But is such a statement actually true? Is scholarship manifest in all publication? Surely such a generalization can be challenged. Being scholarly may mean being involved in research but it does not mean that by definition someone has engaged in scholarship. The end product may not be viewed as achieving scholarship even if the individual has been seen to be scholarly. Therefore, whilst writing for publication could be seen as a scholarly activity and a practice of scholarship, it is not scholarship itself. The increasing plethora of journal articles would not support a notion that scholarship has increased.

The same can be seen with the notion of teaching. Whilst Boyer attempted to include teaching within scholarship, the increasing literature on pedagogy relates it to issues of excellence and defining these as aspects of process. Whilst teachers can engage in scholarly activity, their students can often appear to have learned nothing and may state that they have been taught nothing, implying that the teachers were not teaching but only trying to teach. Hence, teaching may be best described as an attempt to achieve learning which is sometimes successful. Even when teaching is seen as being excellent in practice, and is viewed as such by students, the end product may actually not tally with the concept of the scholarship of teaching. For this the teaching would need to be viewed beyond the mere process of what happened and reflect on the reasons why learning has occurred. A judgement about excellent teaching usually gets little further than the first aspect, a view of the process.

Elton (1992) argues that scholarship should be at the heart of both teaching and research. In relation to teaching, scholarship should be defined in terms not just of what happens and the activities related to it but of how it happens. This reiterates a problem identified by Passmore (1980): that many are still attracted by the notion that it is the knowing *what* that is crucial to being an effective teacher – a view that is potentially limiting in any attempt to define scholarship. Whilst scholarship suggests a deep conceptual understanding of academic work, this alternative view suggests a narrow and discipline-orientated approach. This could be seen to have trapped Boyer. As we have seen, he suggested four areas of scholarship: discovery; integration; application; and teaching. Why stop here? Why is there not a scholarship of assessment, for example? Boyer's suggestion could be interpreted as a process model. Scholarship starts with discovery; this then becomes integrated within disciplines, where it is applied; then it is taught to others. This formulation is the basis for another cyclical model to add to those already in the educational literature (see Figure 3.2). Boyer's definition also highlights a division of scholarship into research and teaching components. The knowledge component, however, could be seen as integral to both, so why separate this out?

Scholarship pervades the work of academics in both their research and their teaching. It is about the beliefs and values that attach to such

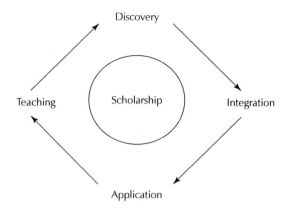

*Figure 3.2*

virtues. Although some of these values may be refracted through the lens of a discipline, they come from the concept of scholarship and not the other way around. Values and beliefs that define scholarship adapt to the discipline and are qualified by it.

## The problem with excellence

When trying to define scholarship in relation to teaching and learning a significant distraction is caused by the growing literature in higher education that concentrates upon techniques and 'tips' for teaching more effectively. Whilst the strategies that are proposed may help to increase student participation and interaction, there is a need to extend beyond mere techniques as they threaten to trivialize the rich and complex relationship between teaching and learning. Only when this relationship is explored is the concept of scholarship examined.

Examining the link between teaching, learning and reflection is becoming difficult as the notion of scholarship becomes increasingly linked to the notion of excellence and the setting of standards. A logical progression of this in the UK would see the Higher Education Academy create a set of criteria upon which higher education will be able to evaluate teaching. The recent DfES paper *The Future of Higher Education* (2003) notes that 'all providers should set down their expectations of teachers with reference to national professional standards' and the Higher Education Academy has prepared a framework of national standards (HEA 2004).

This is not a new agenda in the UK or Australia. The work of the Institute for Learning and Teaching in Higher Education (ILTHE) in the UK reflects the development of this agenda. An additional criterion was recently added to the entry route for experienced staff. Applicants are now expected, in the terms used on the application form, to show the 'integration of scholarship, research and professional activities' within their teaching. In addition, as part of the application there is the suggestion that a stated professional value is the 'commitment to scholarship in teaching, both generally and within their own discipline' (http://www.ilt.ac.uk).

Using scholarship in such a way suggests that teaching can be defined as a set of processes. This has been taken forward by notions of excellence in teaching which miss a stage by not conceptualizing what the process is; scholarship becomes merely the demonstration of these processes which leads to excellence. As a result the scholarship of teaching is viewed as the end result of a process but not a concept. It suggests that at a certain point academics cross a line and have achieved scholarship (Figure 3.3). Following this process model suggests that people can be excellent teachers but have no notion of the scholarship of teaching at all. This distinction has been used as a way of differentiating between the competence that all should demonstrate and the scholarship that only those applying themselves to real understanding will achieve.

This may have been what Kreber (2002) was explaining when she said that there is a difference between 'excellent teachers' and 'expert teachers'. Echoing the work of the Carnegie Institute, she proposes that a scholar is someone who shares their knowledge and advances the knowledge of teaching and learning within their discipline in a transparent way that can be 'peer-reviewed'. This hints at the view of early philosophers, that the enlightened have a moral responsibility

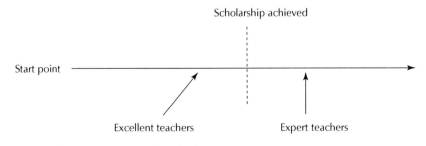

*Figure 3.3* The development of scholarship

to share understanding with others. However, for it to be scholarship it must be transparent and available to peers, to those in the discipline and to the public alike.

Kreber feels that despite advances in our understanding of the scholarship of teaching there is still no unified definition. As a result there is little acceptance of how the notion relates to other phenomena or to scholarship itself. This is perhaps not surprising if the scholarship of teaching has been viewed as the end result of a range of processes that are not clearly perceived as being underpinned by conceptual understanding. Although many academics are excellent teachers and can describe what they do, there is less understanding of why they do what they do or what this is based upon. Knowledge about teaching is constructed in different ways: by formal research; from the literature; through practice and experience. It is the latter that is usually seen as the crucial element in achieving excellence but this may help to create some of the confusion. The emphasis remains on what people have done or do and not on asking themselves why they are undertaking this. Kreber and Cranton (2000) argue that the scholarship of teaching includes learning about teaching and then demonstrating that knowledge in the teaching environment. They envisage a more holistic approach to explaining the scholarship of teaching. During her research Kreber noted that academics did not feel that everybody who teaches should be expected to practise the scholarship of teaching. Would they say the same in relation to research? It is this regularly returned-to debate that now needs to be considered.

## Research versus teaching

Braxton et al. (2002) found, perhaps not surprisingly, that the scholarship of discovery is seen as the most 'legitimate' form of scholarship. The danger is that scholarship becomes subsumed as part of research, and yet surely research represents a form of scholarship, as does teaching. The drawing of these boundaries continues to cause some difficulties. Boyer attempted to move us away from such discussions by suggesting that the teaching versus research debate is old and should not take up precious energy. He argues that the concept of scholarship should be seen as relating to all areas of the work of an academic.

The research versus teaching debate does, however, provide some ideas that may be worth being distracted by. Research and notions of scholarship focus on conceiving answers by finding problems and issues that have no explanation as yet. The key to high-quality research is shedding light where there is currently darkness. In teaching, the notion of a problem is usually not the basis upon which a practitioner begins. The emphasis of the literature is on avoiding the notion of difficulty or problem within the learning environment. As Jarvis (1999) found, we tend to highlight what has 'gone wrong' in our teaching and seek to prevent this occurring by consulting the literature before it occurs. He argues that we need to pose questions to solve if we are to develop our teaching and therefore to understand it rather than merely to be provided with answers. This requires thinking about teaching and then asking the relevant questions to solve the identified problems. As stated earlier in the chapter, this approach requires teaching to be reflected upon before, during and after the actual practice. Within high-quality research, people question throughout. They stop and think about their results before presenting them, and the presentation of results is an enhancement of the process of investigation. This facilitates deeper understanding. Can we see teaching as the same? Shulman argues that at present we cannot. Reflection and analysis are crucial but often do not occur. The danger of the most recent policy documentation is that the questioning approach crucial to scholarship is not encouraged.

For scholarship to be recognized within teaching, the definitions need to incorporate what is not known, what is to be discovered. Boyer's classification may appear to take this as a separate feature relating to research alone. Perhaps this in hindsight perpetuates the divide that he wanted the academic community to abandon by suggesting that the scholarship of teaching is at the end of a continuum that begins with discovery or 'research'. According to Andresen (2000: 25), 'Research as such is merely one specialised, bounded and distinctive area within scholarship.' He goes on to argue that the scholarship related to the researcher is mostly about investigation whereas the scholarship of teaching is about being aggregative and interpretive. The necessary relationship that exists between teaching and research is through scholarship. A teacher needs to be able to build up research about the learning that is taking place and to remain in touch with all that he or she is engaged with. This, in Andresen's view, is not the same as being a researcher. The researcher does not need to care. A teacher needs to be able to transform and enable and make accessible in a way that a researcher does not. The implications of this argument are that to be a high-quality teacher one does need to be a high-quality researcher. Both need to be scholars if they are to create scholarship in either guise.

# The need to reconceptualize scholarship

The work of scholars since Aristotle has shown us that scholarship is about discovery, and this element has always been associated with the definition. However, the definition does not and should not stop at this point. The contraction in meaning that has occurred has led to confusion and an opportunity for other definitions to become established. As the work of those in the professions has been called more into question and scrutiny has grown, the role of defining terms and values has become less obvious. Whilst academics may have had freedom in centuries past to contemplate their role and deliver definition and meaning as a result, the postmodern state no longer allows the academic such space. The result has been that whilst academics have argued and hypothesized about the meaning of scholarship and debated whether the definition provides sufficient understanding of related terms such as 'the scholarship of teaching', the policy agenda has taken over and begun to fill the void. This agenda has even enticed some academics to engage in these debates. The danger of such an approach can be seen if we consider the argument put forward by Bertrand Russell (1956) about logic and knowledge. Russell suggested that the names that are commonly used are really just abbreviations for descriptions, so that when a word is used, such as 'scholarship', it actually acts as a description of what that means by relating it to connected thoughts. If Russell is correct, the problem for our understanding of scholarship is that these abbreviations initially became constricted so that they related to research alone. Now that the abbreviations are opening up again they are doing so without providing a real understanding. Wittgenstein in his *Philosophical Investigations* provides us with an explanation for this. He argues that what makes a description current is the understanding that is brought to it by the community concerned. As outlined above, this community is no longer exclusively those drawn from the academic community. The community that corroborates the current meaning associated with the term 'scholarship' is now drawn from the ranks of those forming and driving the policy agenda, supported by some academics.

The policy initiatives are not driven by a desire to understand the terms and the theoretical underpinnings of the work of academics and therefore by definition to improve learning. They are driven by the intention of enhancing and improving teaching and learning. They lean on terms such as 'the scholarship of teaching' and ally these to notions of excellence and quality. These definitions relate to the outcomes of the work of the scholar and are associated with process. The conceptualization of scholarship requires the definition to begin *before* the process starts. Only at this stage is the scholar involved in learning from both his or her own perspective and that of the student or public. Scholarship needs to reconceptualized so that real meaning is given to all the associated terms that it relates to. This reconceptualization needs to be driven by the academy and not to limit itself to the processes involved. The meaning of scholarship needs to be given clarity and then the related terms, such as the 'scholarship of teaching', can be grounded in reality and provide meaning that will support the understanding of scholarship.

*Chapter 4*

# Scholarship of teaching: an emerging concept

We know what we are, but know not what we may be.
(William Shakespeare)

Much of the research cited in this chapter was conducted prior to the introduction of the UK Higher Education Academy (HEA) in 2004 and the integration of the Institute for Learning and Teaching in Higher Education (ILTHE) into the HEA. The pace of change and the need to reconsider aspects of the enhancement agenda within the United Kingdom have not diminished; one could argue that they have increased. A consultation paper on the future of professional standards has now been issued and the accreditation of teaching and learning programmes is administered through a set of criteria and values, one of which is 'the scholarship of teaching'. The arguments put forward in this chapter remain pertinent to any discussion on the scholarship of teaching, its meaning, its conceptualization and its interpretation by academics and the academic community as a whole.

The preceding chapters have shown how and why the term 'scholarship' needs to be reconsidered and placed within a conceptual context that takes account of historical, philosophical and sociological factors that have determined the evolution of the term. This chapter demonstrates how the word 'scholarship' with respect to teaching has become confused and misplaced and used to sustain and enhance a particular type of credibility in activities related to the enhancement of learning and teaching in higher education. Bourdieu's concept of symbolic culture is used to construct the argument and show how the use of the phrase 'scholarship of teaching' needs to be re-examined and reconceptualized. Twenty-five academics from a variety of disciplines were interviewed about their perceptions of scholarship, the scholarship of teaching, and scholarship in teaching. These data were used to develop a framework for understanding and possibly reconsidering the role of the scholarship of teaching.

## Establishing the context

Within the United Kingdom the Institute for Learning and Teaching (ILT) was created to help enhance teaching and learning within higher education (Dearing Report 1997). Part of the ILT's remit was to develop accredited programmes in teaching and learning for lecturers in higher education. The ILT had five core elements, one of which was 'Professional Values'; within this category it stated that members and associates of the institute would be expected to adhere to the professional value of 'a commitment to scholarship in teaching both generally and within their own discipline'. What does this mean? Increasingly the ILT, Educational Development Units (EDU), and Staff Development and Training Units (SDTU) have linked the word 'scholarship' to teaching as a means of raising the status and credibility of the programmes that are run or accredited. I would like to argue that this is ill advised and detrimental to enhancing learning and teaching in higher education. Scholarship is an abstract term, particularly when used without context.

The argument is divided into three sections. First, I consider Boyer's (1990) notions of the scholarship of teaching and what these might mean to an academic and the academic community. Boyer's (1990) work is used as a means of underpinning the principal notions and concepts attached to the scholarship of teaching. This is an important aspect of the argument as it shows how present misconceptions surrounding the scholarship of teaching have pushed the discussion towards an expectation that academics will adhere to a professional value of scholarship in teaching which, I contend, hinders teaching and learning within the academic community.

The second part of the argument concentrates on Bourdieu's (1986, 1988, 1989) principles of symbolic culture and social capital. I argue that an individual or sets of individuals can try to enhance the status of various activities by using terminology that is recognized and accepted by a particular audience. I suggest that in this case the

ILT, EDUs and SDTUs are using the language of scholarship within an academic discourse as a means of promoting teaching and learning within the academic community and giving teaching greater symbolic capital. Introducing the notion of scholarship in/of teaching into the vocabulary of an academic community that generally associates scholarship with research and intellectual activity does not help the enhancement of teaching and learning. Such an approach has created confusion within the academic community's understanding of scholarship and its role within teaching and learning.

The final section of the argument analyses the research data and provides an insight into academics' perception of the term 'scholarship' and the concept of the scholarship of teaching. A structured questionnaire was issued to twenty-five academics to assess what they understood by scholarship and the scholarship of teaching. Each participant was asked to join an interdisciplinary focus group to further explore the notion of scholarship. The findings from the focus groups were used to compare individual responses with group responses. This chapter concentrates on individual responses from sample academics in the Humanities, Physical and Health Sciences, Medicine and Management.

## Defining scholarship

Scholarship can be defined in a variety of ways depending on the purpose of the definition. For example, a major grant-awarding body in the USA states that:

> 'Scholarship' may be defined as any activity of 'critical, systematic investigation in one or more fields and the submission of one's findings for criticism by professional peers and the public through published writings, lectures, or other modes of presentation.'
>
> Scholarship has also been defined as having three key characteristics: it should be public, susceptible to critical review and evaluation and accessible for exchange and use by other members of one's scholarly community.
>
> (Shulman 1998)

These definitions are very pragmatic and are aimed at assisting those dealing with achievable outcomes from research. However, scholarship can be considered from two alternative viewpoints: polemic scholarship, which promotes a particular position, is specifically designed to advance a cause; and academic scholarship, which is neutral and has no particular aim other than finding out the truth (Shulman 1987). Both forms are commonly referred to as scholarship and consequently many misunderstandings occur, as in the scholarship of teaching (Paulsen and Feldman 1995). The difference in approach between polemic and academic scholarship helps in the analysis of definitions of scholarship given by the research sample, as well as providing insight into the confusion and misunderstandings related to the Scholarship of Teaching.

Polemic scholarship tends to research texts. In other words, it looks at evidence within the discipline and rarely goes outside the discipline. It hopes to find all the answers to whatever question is being asked within the disciplinary texts themselves. For example, in Law a particular case may be compared with many similar cases within one judicial system, but not looked at from outside this context for a different perspective. Polemic scholarship is very introspective and might be thought of as simplistic in its approach. Academic scholarship, on the other hand, allows explanations to be found through exploring all angles, but particularly areas outside the immediate field. Again taking Law as our example, academic scholarship would compare cases from a variety of cultures, contexts and judicial boundaries, e.g. the European Court of Law as opposed to a single European nation's judicial system.

## Boyer's Scholarship reconsidered

Ernest Boyer (1990) in his work *Scholarship Revisited* was one of the first to draw attention to the narrow conception of scholarship held by the academic profession. He states that:

> Scholarship is not an esoteric appendage; it is at the heart of what the profession is all about. All faculty, throughout their careers, should themselves remain students. As scholars they must continue to learn and be seriously and continuously engaged in the expanding intellectual world. This is essential to the vitality and vigour of the undergraduate college.
>
> (p. 36)

Boyer observes that academics traditionally see three components in their work: scholarship, teaching and service. He suggests that although these three components are related, for many purposes the academic community treats them as separate. For example, when an academic is considered for promotion, each of the three components is evaluated separately. Boyer suggests that dividing the academic's professional life in this way is misleading. Instead, he argues that academics are first, foremost and perhaps exclusively scholars. However, he does not associate scholarship solely with research and creative activity; he sees scholarship as encompassing all the traditional roles of an academic.

Boyer's analysis of scholarship identifies four key roles: discovery, integration, application and teaching. He considers teaching not simply as a matter of dissemination and the transmission of knowledge, but as a form of scholarship. By this he means the transformation and extension of knowledge through the process of classroom debate and a continual examination and challenge of both content and pedagogy.

Before considering the implications of Boyer's four forms of scholarship, it is important to reflect on Boyer's own beliefs:

> We acknowledge that these four – the scholarship of discovery, of integration, of application and of teaching – divide intellectual functions that are tied inseparably to each other. Still there is value, we believe, in analysing the various kinds of academic work, while also acknowledging that they dynamically interact, formatting an independent whole.
>
> (Boyer 1990: 25)

This assertion enables us to look at scholarship in a broader context, thus allowing it to be viewed as an interrelated whole with distinctive components and different approaches to knowing.

## The four forms of scholarship

Boyer's first form of scholarship was the 'scholarship of discovery', which relates to the discovery of new empirical data or creating novel artistic forms. The scholarship of discovery equates closely to the traditional mission of research activity. Boyer emphasized that the scholarship of discovery, or research, is a 'pervasive process of intellectual excitement' rather than just a concern with outcomes in the form of new knowledge. He also realized that the extension of the frontiers of knowledge was not enough, and that academics need to be constantly involved in the interpretation of knowledge. His second category, the 'scholarship of integration', relates to the interpretation given to emergent data or new artistic forms as they are integrated with other results and compared to other creations. This allows academics to make connections between knowledge and models gained from different disciplines. It requires a divergent approach to knowing. The 'scholarship of application', Boyer's third type, was defined as professional activity in practice and service, which had to be subject to the rigour of evaluation and accountability as teaching and research.

Finally, and most important, is the 'scholarship of teaching'. Boyer suggests that the scholarship of teaching has integrity of its own, but is deeply embedded in the other three forms. The particular characteristics are first, its *synoptic capacity*, the ability to draw the strands of a field together in a way that provides both coherence and meaning. Second, *pedagogical content knowledge*, the capacity to represent a subject in ways that transcend the split between intellectual substance and teaching process. Third, *what we know about learning*, scholarly enquiry into how students 'make meaning' out of what teachers say and do.

Boyer's view of the scholarship of teaching was as an inclusive activity. This perspective suggests that academics should take a scholarly approach to teaching by reflecting on the knowledge gained from educational research in relation to particular contexts in which they teach. It emphasizes the important reciprocal relationship that exists between theory and practice, and the value of practitioners' experienced-based knowledge. Boyer was quite explicit in his understanding of the concept of the 'scholarship of teaching', but his untimely death left the concept open to examination and reinterpretation. A consequence of this has been that the last decade has seen an increased interest in the notion and interpretation of the scholarship of teaching (Prosser et al. 1994, Kember 1997, Kreber 1999, 2000, 2002b, Kreber and Cranton 2000, Trigwell et al. 2000).

## The scholarship of teaching

Two major studies have recently tried to contextualize the scholarship of teaching (Trigwell et al. 2000, Kreber 2002b). Trigwell et al. suggest that there are five qualitatively different, hierarchical interpretations of the scholarship of teaching which move from what the teacher does to a focus on student learning. According to Trigwell they differ in four dimensions: the source of *information* teachers draw upon; the focus of their *reflection*; the nature and extent of their *communication* of insights; and their *conceptions of teaching* and learning. The model put forward suggests that to engage in higher-order activities within the scholarship of teaching requires academics to consult discipline-specific literature on teaching and learning, focus reflection on specific areas of one's practice, focus teaching on students and learning, and publish results of teaching initiatives through peer-review mechanisms. As a consequence academic staff can engage in the scholarship of teaching to varying degrees.

Kreber (2002a) suggests that there are four distinct areas, the first of which proposes that the scholarship of teaching is a product of the scholarship of discovery, i.e. that the scholarship of teaching can be found in books, articles and peer-reviewed conferences on teaching (Healey 2000, Richlin 2001). The second dimension suggests that the scholarship of teaching is practised by excellent teachers and thus equates scholarship with excellence (Morehead and Shedd 1996). The third area covers the notion that the scholarship of teaching is associated with the knowledge of the expert teacher, and the final dimension concentrates on the teacher's experienced-based knowledge.

Kreber (2002b) contends that

> to some extent the way the scholarship of teaching is conceptualised can be inferred from the context within which the term is used. This is to say that the idea or concept of the scholarship of teaching, when used in the context of raising the quality of teaching and learning within an institution or department, is likely be very different from that underlying intent to give greater weight to teaching in tenure and promotion decisions.
>
> (p. 7)

She concludes by saying that 'the scholarship of teaching despite its long intuitive appeal to many, to date has been a concept lacking a unified definition' (p. 8).

The work of Trigwell et al. (2000) and Kreber (2002b) suggests that a great deal more research is required in this field if the scholarship of teaching is to have clear, distinct and definitive meaning for the academic community. It is a concept than can have powerful meaning, but its present lack of definition is causing confusion within the community and allows other agencies to use the term as a power base to enhance teaching and learning in higher education. Within any community, communication of ideas is a key aspect of understanding and concept building; higher education is no exception. Understanding how the scholarship of teaching is used in higher education and in particular by agencies associated with higher education, such as the ILT, requires a theoretical framework. Social theory and in particular concepts such as social, cultural and symbolic capital offer a framework in which to explore the power base of terms such as 'the scholarship of teaching'.

## Social capital and cultural capital

Social capital is generally defined as a form of social behaviour which is found amongst cohesive groups and communities where reciprocity and mutuality form the basis of informal communication. Collective interests and mutual trust create a kind of interdependence where each member absorbs and understands the unwritten rules of behaviour of that social entity. Wann (1995) suggests that social capital is a form of social wealth that provides what the market cannot. In this sense social capital has economic value. It is a non-market-driven means of exchanging 'knowledge skills and power' (p. 103) and of managing unpredictability by relying on spontaneous responses to local situations generated through the ethos of self-help (Preece and Houghton 2000). This is an important aspect when we are considering how the term 'scholarship of teaching' has been introduced to the academic community in England. The ILT introduced scholarship in teaching as a professional value, thus trying to raise the social and economic value of teaching within a community that prizes highly the notion of scholarship as represented by Boyer's scholarship of discovery. Etzioni (1995) suggests this comes about by communities' 'interpersonal bonds to encourage members to abide by shared values' (p. ix). The difficulty with Etzioni's model of community is the implicit assumption that communities are homogeneous and that one community's concept of 'civil and moral order' is the same as another's. Etzioni's perspective helps to shed light on why there is so much confusion within the academic community about the notion of the scholarship of teaching. To propose that the scholarship in/of teaching can be a professional value assumes a great deal about the higher-education community. But the higher-education community is not homogeneous, nor is its civil and moral order. Fukuyama (1995) suggests that trust, which emanates from shared values, has a 'measurable economic value' (p. 10). He avoids the problem of differential values between social groups by suggesting that there are some core societal values which individuals with high social capital can draw on, thus enabling them to 'form new associations and operate in several different groups' (p. 27). This last aspect of Fukuyama's hypothesis sheds light on why the term 'scholarship in/of teaching' has been used by national agencies in trying to raise the profile and status of teaching. Based on Fukuyama's description of high social capital, the ILT's core-values approach to raising the status of teaching was ill conceived.

## Establishing the role of the ILT

It is essential to understand the role of the ILT and why it plays a significant part in my arguments. The ILT was set up as a professional body to recognize the work of higher-education staff involved in teaching and the support of learning. The ILT had three main functions:

- accreditation of training programmes for higher-education teachers
- research and development in teaching and learning
- stimulation of innovation.

The ILT membership criteria required individuals to be informed by underpinning knowledge and professional values including commitments to learning and scholarship as an integral part of teaching. Appendix 1 of the ILT's document on accreditation stated that: 'Courses seeking accreditation should be designed with an awareness of the core knowledge and professional values that are expected of members of the Institute for Learning and Teaching in Higher Education'. Members of the ILT were expected to adhere to the following professional values:

- a commitment to scholarship in teaching, both generally and within their own discipline
- respect for individual learners and for their development and empowerment
- a commitment to the development of learning communities, including students, teachers and all those engaged in learning support
- a commitment to encouraging participation in higher education and to equality of educational opportunity
- a commitment to continued reflection and evaluation and consequent improvement of their own practice.

Each of the above values has implications for the academic (Nicholls 2000, 2001, Nicholls and Jarvis 2002). I am particularly interested in the first value – commitment to scholarship in teaching. There is a difference between the discourse and language of the scholarship *of* teaching as suggested by Boyer and scholarship *in* teaching as put forward by the ILT. It is necessary to understand why such a difference is important, and the implications for teaching and learning within the academic community. Bourdieu's concept of cultural capital helps define the problem in relation to the scholarship of teaching as a mechanism for promoting teaching in academic discourse. How cultural capital is conceptualized can also be used to structure new ways of considering the role of scholarship in the academic community.

## Bourdieu's notions of symbolic capital and cultural capital

For Bourdieu (1993, 1994) culture, while being autonomous on one level, is also arbitrary and bears within it the voice of power – that is, the power to impose classifications. Symbolic power nevertheless does not happen without some compliance by social actors. It must have a resonance in a *habitus*, a form of life.

> Symbolic violence is that particular form of constraint that can only be implemented with the active complicity – which does not mean that it is conscious and voluntary – of those who submit to it and are determined only insofar as they deprive themselves of the possibility of a freedom founded on the awakening of consciousness.
>
> (Bourdieu 1994: 4)

Bourdieu's term 'misrecognition' (*méconnaissance*) is useful to the argument I am making in relation to the scholarship of teaching. He employs the term to mean false consciousness, that is, the cognitive ability of the dominant culture (such as the ILT's use of the term 'scholarship') to disguise the social conditions of its existence by falsely giving itself the status of something natural and legitimate.

It is a central tenet of Bourdieu's sociology (Bourdieu and Wacquant 1992) that culture exists as a cognitive system offering groups the means of imposing and maintaining classifications. This is what constitutes Bourdieu's cultural capital, which has two elements: symbolic and material capital. The former refers to cultural resources, such as status, prestige and various kinds of cultural distinctiveness; the latter is largely concerned with inherent wealth.

Cultural capital is identified as a complex array of educational qualifications and forms of cultural differentiation in terms of language and general proximity to knowledge of cultural institutions. However, cultural capital cannot simply be thought of as cultural 'objects' to be acquired or possessed.

> Cultural capital can exist in three forms: in the embodied state, i.e. in the form of long-standing dispositions of the mind and body; in the objectified state, in the form of cultural goods (pictures, books, dictionaries, instruments, machines, etc.) . . . and in the institutional state, a form of objectification, which must be apart because, as will be seen in the case of educational qualifications, it confers entirely original properties on the cultural capital which it is presumed to guarantee.
>
> (Bourdieu 1986: 243)

Agents are positioned within a social field by virtue of their total accumulation of symbolic capital, which is gained from any combination of economic, cultural and social capital. Power within a field is ultimately gained by the possession of symbolic capital. The site of struggle within fields is, however, not just over possession of capital but over the very definition of what capital is at stake and what is valued. In this sense capital is arbitrary and the determination of what capital is valued is constantly being defined and redefined (Delanty 2001, Boudon 1986). Using the term 'scholarship' in conjunction with teaching can be considered as a form of capital that can gain value and be valued by those who engage in teaching, and thus raise the status of teaching.

Symbolic capital is primarily cognitive (Bourdieu and Wacquant 1992, Bourdieu 1998). It is power that is recognized as having an intrinsic value of itself. In this sense, the cognitive dimension of symbolic capital is less a form of consciousness than it is a cultural disposition. A good example of this is the ILT teaching fellowships. These were created to give high national stature to academics who excelled in teaching and innovation in teaching. Each successful applicant received significant financial support to conduct further research and development within teaching and learning. This emulates the cultural disposition of research scholarships and awards, and thus attempts to give teaching greater symbolic capital within the academic community.

These examples highlight the need for those engaged in higher education to have a better understanding and conceptualization of the scholarship of teaching, particularly for those involved in teaching in higher education. The empirical data collected for this article have concentrated on academics within the higher-education community in the United Kingdom, but have taken account of previous studies in the field, which have been predominantly conducted in North America and Australia (Andresen 2000, Trigwell et al. 2000, Kreber 2002a).

## Exploring academics' perceptions of the scholarship of teaching

The research reported here analyses the perceptions and conceptions of academics from different disciplines of the notions of scholarship and the scholarship of teaching. Most had a clear perception and conception of what scholarship is and how it relates to their particular discipline. They attempt to identify scholarship within their own discipline as well as assess its possible value and meaning. The most interesting data relate to their views of the scholarship of teaching and where, if at all, it fits into their understanding of scholarship within their domain. Bourdieu's description of academic *habitus* guides the conclusions of the research findings by suggesting that the use of terms such as 'the scholarship of/in teaching' is a means of gaining symbolic and cultural capital for those who wish to promote teaching for their own gain and status rather than for a true enhancement of learning activities in higher education.

## Research methodology

Twenty-five academics, varying in discipline, age and status, were interviewed through a semi-structured interview as a means of identifying their perceptions and conceptions of scholarship and the scholarship of teaching. The sample of academics comprised two senior professors from Law, two senior professors and two new lecturers from Health and Life Sciences, one professor and one experienced academic from Psychiatry, three experienced academics from Management, five from Medicine, three from Education, three from Biomedical Sciences, and three from Humanities. Each was asked five open questions:

1. What do you understand by the term Scholarship?
2. What do you perceive the scholarship of your discipline to be?
3. What do you understand by the Scholarship of Teaching?
4. Do you think there is a Scholarship of Teaching?
5. If yes, what does the Scholarship of Teaching constitute for you?

The interviews were recorded and transcribed for analysis. All participants were volunteers and complete anonymity has been observed. The analysis of the data was conducted through coding data sets and comparing data sets from a perspective of age, gender, status and discipline.

## Understanding and defining the term 'scholarship'

Initial analysis was aimed at deriving a common understanding of the term 'scholarship'. Definitions were categorized in the first instance into sets of common terms. These included: problem solving, critical thinking and production of new knowledge. At this stage of the analysis, the data sets were not considered from a perspective of meaning (i.e. what does critical thinking mean to a scientist or one who is engaged in humanities?). The categorization was produced as a means of interrogating the data further and of ascribing meaning to those disciplines involved in the study. From this initial analysis a very clear set of generic terms emerged in relation to the definitions of 'scholarship' as a concept, which was independent of age, gender and discipline. All respondents were articulate and specific in their interpretations of the term 'scholarship'. This clarity was demonstrated by an overwhelming agreement that scholarship required:

- a critical mind to be brought to ideas and concepts
- the ability to synthesize and problem-solve based on evidence
- a capacity to take a long-term view
- a clear and deep understanding and conceptualization of one's subject area
- producing new knowledge and perspectives
- facilitating the understanding of new knowledge by a variety of audiences, including peers
- disseminating new knowledge through a variety of avenues.

Scholarship appeared to be founded on three basic principles:

- critical thinking and problem-solving
- production, conceptualization and understanding of new knowledge
- dissemination of knowledge to a variety of audiences.

The most interesting aspect of these classifications is that in each of the three areas participants stressed that scholarship required the academic to ensure that a variety of audiences understood the new knowledge. When probed further, it was clear that the respondents perceived communication of new knowledge as a key aspect of scholarship. In conjunction with the need to disseminate knowledge was a strong conviction that scholarship was not just about know-ledge production, but about understanding, problem-solving and conceptualizing issues from a broad perspective. This perception of scholarship can be aligned to the 'academic' definition of scholarship rather than a 'polemic' or practical definition.

## Understanding the meaning of scholarship within disciplines

Exploring the generic interpretation of scholarship revealed many similarities in conceptions, as described above. However, when asked for an understanding or definition of scholarship within a discipline, the academics revealed significant differences. Comparison of the data sets showed that academics from similar disciplines held common perceptions and understandings related to their field. For example, in Law, scholarship was connected both to advocacy and practice, i.e. what Law does and the study of Law. There was agreement that scholarship in Law came from having time to research, analyse and synthesize problems and most importantly to provide critical objec-tivity. In Management scholarship was perceived as different from research but included research. Scholarship was seen as entailing engagement with ideas and being creative in the formulation of new and dynamic alternatives to established methodologies and processes. In the Health and Life Sciences, equating scholarship to academic excellence, which reflects depth of knowledge and understanding in a particular field, was a recurring theme. In the Health and Life Sciences, as with Medicine, scholarship related to the ability to solve problems, discover new treatments/processes and disseminate such findings to peers. Peer acceptance was a dominant factor of scholarship. Understanding the need for process such as the experimental method and the equivalent need to exemplify the process was a high prerequisite of scholarship in the scientific disciplines.

## Understandings of the term 'Scholarship of Teaching'

The following three questions were asked:

1. What do you understand by the Scholarship of Teaching?
2. Do you think there is a Scholarship of Teaching?
3. If yes what does the Scholarship of Teaching constitute for you?

Academics found these difficult to answer, mainly because most academics do not associate teaching with scholarship. The quotations below exemplify this lack of understanding and confirm both Trigwell's and Kreber's findings. The quotes are from both male and female academics, junior and senior staff.

Responses to the first question, 'What do you understand by the Scholarship of Teaching?' included:

'I don't have one, I don't know what it means.'

'I don't understand what it means – in a broad sense I suppose it could mean using scholarly methods to develop systems of teaching.'

'Means nothing at all, it has been created to take away non-research linked activities of academics.'

'Scholarship is related to intellectual activities that universities are involved in apart from teaching, hence the concept of the scholarship of teaching has no meaning to me and is difficult to understand or even conceptualise.'

Interestingly, most of the respondents (20) said that the notion of 'the scholarship of teaching' is one that they are not familiar with and therefore have not embraced. The participants were also asked whether they saw any difference between 'the scholarship of teaching' and 'scholarship in teaching'. The predominant answer was no, but 18 also suggested it was a matter of semantics and that the notion of scholarship and teaching was one that they were not comfortable with. Two participants (female) did suggest that the difference between the terms was possibly related to how a knowledge of one's own discipline was used to teach undergraduates.

The second and third questions asked: 'Do you think there is a Scholarship of Teaching and if yes what does the Scholarship of Teaching constitute for you?' The responses ranged from a definite NO to 'If I don't understand what the concept is or means, how can it influence my teaching?'. However, there was a difference in the responses from new and longstanding academic staff. New staff were prepared to reflect on the possible meanings and give examples of what might constitute the scholarship of teaching and scholarship in teaching. For example, scholarship of teaching was concerned with how student learning might be improved through a variety of teaching strategies. Scholarship in teaching was thought of as a discipline-based notion, e.g. how to use the latest research findings in undergraduate lectures. The examples given seemed to be based on individual reflections rather than an understanding of the terms.

A senior and eminent professor, on reflection, suggested, 'the scholarship of teaching might relate to the link between teaching and research'. He elaborated this statement by saying: 'the academic who is an expert in a subject area must also have an understanding of teaching and the learning context, in order to ensure that students gain greater depth of understanding'. He made a direct link between the scholarship of teaching and the notion of 'being a good scholar'.

## Conclusions

The chapter has focused on academics' perceptions and conceptions of scholarship, the scholarship of teaching, and the relationship these terms had to their work. Even though the academics interviewed were explicit in their understandings and conceptualization of the term 'scholarship', they were very unsure as to the meaning of the term 'scholarship of teaching' or 'scholarship in teaching'.

On the basis of these findings it is difficult to understand how the higher-education community can accept scholarship in teaching, as suggested by the ILTHE, as being a core professional value. I do not suggest that scholarship in teaching is not a legitimate concept, nor that it should not be valued, but a common understanding of what such a core value might mean to the academic community must be a key starting point. Clearly institutionalizing the scholarship of/in teaching as a core value would require it to be practised, accepted and rewarded within the academic community. For this to occur there must be a broad understanding of the scholarship of/in teaching and what it is to be engaged with it.

This research suggests that there is a need to understand why the concept of the scholarship of/in teaching has gained prominence with agencies such as the ILT. The underlying theoretical framework has been derived from Bourdieu's notions of social, cultural and symbolic capital, and contextualized using Boyer's four forms of scholarship. The argument put forward suggested that using the term 'scholarship' in association with teaching could be a mechanism for promoting teaching in an academic discourse. Using a term such as 'scholarship', which is well understood and conceptualized by academics, in conjunction with teaching gives symbolic capital to teaching, thus raising its status and social capital for those promoting the scholarship of/in teaching as a core professional value.

Analysis of the data suggests that there is a very low level of understanding relating to the term 'scholarship of/in teaching'. Based on this finding it is possible to argue that the scholarship of teaching as a core professional value should be reconsidered. This does not imply that the scholarship of/in teaching as a core professional value is unworthy of consideration. Further research is required in order to understand why the academic community does not embrace the concept of the scholarship of teaching. The current discourse on the scholarship of/in teaching is, as the data suggest, poorly conceptualized and misplaced, serving only to confuse academics' engagement in the enhancement of teaching and learning within the disciplines of the higher-education community. Yet the term 'scholarship of teaching' could offer academics and the academic community a mechanism for exploring teaching and learning in a more systematic and fundamental way, as suggested by Boyer in *Scholarship Reconsidered* (1990).

The lack of conceptualization is widespread, as the research evidence shows (Trigwell et al. 2000 and Kreber 2002a). What is interesting to examine further is why the disciplines hold such firm views about research, scholarship, learning and teaching, and why it is that the disciplines continue to maintain such a firm hold on the academic community and influence thinking in all areas of development, particularly in terms of scholarship, teaching methodologies and concepts of learning. The nature of disciplines and their function in maintaining disciplinary boundaries and strongholds is the focus of the next chapter. Understanding learning and the influence this may have on scholarship is a key aspect of any discussion relating to the disciplines.

# Chapter 5

# Disciplines and scholarship: challenging the power

> Humanity's ever-growing store of knowledge and the fact that each person is bestowed with a unique set of aptitudes leaves most scholars and artists stranded in ever-shrinking islands of competence.
>
> (Cummings 1989)

## What do we mean by discipline?

> A serious lack of discipline in the use of terminology has hampered progress in analysing the sociology of interdisciplinary and multidisciplinary organizations. There is no agreement on what a discipline is let alone what distinguishes terms such as inter-, multi, or cross-disciplinary from each other.
>
> (Roy 1979: 169)

When the implications of the nature and contexts of disciplines within teaching and learning are being discussed, it is essential to consider what the term 'discipline' may mean. Attempts to define it are often plagued by institutional particularity about individual turf, academic goals, student needs, pedagogical philosophies, administrative curricular policies, and attitudes towards nonmainstream curricula (Glasgow 1997: xxiv). Disciplinarity has had a profound effect on the generation and transmission of knowledge and as a consequence has multiple meanings. For example, discipline implies both a domain to be investigated and the methods used in that domain (Pfnister 1969: 25). The term denotes exclusivity; it is used to distinguish one body of knowledge from another, emphasizing primarily characteristics that separate discrete units of knowledge as opposed to those that might relate them (Swoboda 1979: 64). Kockelmans (1979) defines discipline as 'a branch of learning or a field of study characterised by a body of intersubjectively acceptable knowledge, pertaining to a well-defined realm of entities, systematically established on the basis of generally accepted principles with the help of methodical rules and procedures: e.g., mathematics, chemistry, and history' (p. 127). A further definition is that of Kiger (1971), who states that a discipline is a 'recognised branch or segment of knowledge within rational learning with certain generally agreed upon canons and standards' (pp. 52–3).

These definitions rely more on the mechanistic meanings of the term, rather than its operational use. Education theory gives another dimension to the meaning of discipline by incorporating an operational context on the basis of organizational structures in higher-education institutions. Davis (1995) defines discipline as a 'discrete subject and its characteristic regimen of investigation and analysis, e.g., geography, political science, psychology, and English'. In most institutions these realms are normally accommodated structurally in departments, which in turn administer the teaching, research and scholarship. As Roy (1979: 163) suggests, 'for all intents and purposes on any one campus, disciplines equate to departments'. Understanding the term 'discipline' is important to any discussion about teaching, learning and scholarship within higher education. Within this context discipline is taken to mean any comparatively self-contained and isolated domain of human experience that possesses its own community of experts.

## Why consider the disciplines?

Within every higher-education institution individual disciplines form the focus of learning; students apply for specific courses, all of which are discipline based, or framed within a specialized context. Disciplines have been, and appear to remain, the mainstay of thinking about learning within the academy. Staff consider themselves as chemists or anthropologists rather than generalized teachers. Studies such as those of Becher (1989) and Hativa and Marincovich (1995) have shown quite clearly how subject specialism and discipline separates the academy. It is interesting to note that Becher (1989), Biglan (1973a, 1973b) and Kolb (1981) group the disciplines under one or other of the broad headings hard pure, soft pure, hard applied and soft applied, each manifesting its own epistemological characteristics. Neumann et al. (2002: 406) summarize these as follows:

- Hard pure knowledge, of which physics and chemistry are exemplars, is typified as having a cumulative, atomistic structure, concerned with universals, simplification and a quantitative emphasis. Knowledge communities tend to be competitive but gregarious: joint or multiple authorship is commonplace.
- Soft pure knowledge, of which history and anthropology offer cases in point, is, in contrast, reiterative, holistic, concerned with particulars, and having a qualitative bias. There is no sense of superseded knowledge, as in hard pure fields. Scholarly enquiry is typically a solitary pursuit, manifesting only a limited overlap of interest between researchers.
- Hard applied knowledge, typified by engineering, derives its underpinnings from hard pure enquiry, is concerned with mastery of the physical environment and geared towards products and techniques.
- Soft applied knowledge, such as education and management studies, in its turn is dependent on soft pure knowledge, being concerned with the enhancement of professional practice and aiming to yield protocols and procedures.

Biglan adds another point to this list:

- Applied knowledge communities, especially hard applied ones, are also gregarious, with multiple influences and interactions on both their teaching and research activity (Biglan 1973b).

This classification has been used to describe both research and teaching within the disciplines. The relationship between the two is reflected in the knowledge base for the curriculum, and thus the content of teaching, which essentially comprises a selection from the body of mainstream research material (Neumann et al. 2002).

The above research and classifications highlight the continuing growth of disciplinary speciality in higher education; they also underscore the need to find meaningful ways to link the disparate and sometimes isolated spheres of academic life. Traditional models of isolated scholarship have become central to the intellectual work of the academy (Astin and Baldwin 1991, Benowitz 1995, Newell and Klein 1999) and academic interaction across disciplinary boundaries does not happen very often. In other words the disciplines function very much within what Becher (1989) describes as academic tribes and territories. Some scholars have described distinct patterns of attitudes, meanings and behaviours relating to disciplines, institutions, the professions and even national systems (Dill 1991, Tierney and Rhoads 1994).

These various aspects of culture within higher education exert powerful influences on academics. In both the UK and the USA, attitudes and behaviours relating to disciplinary orientation seem to dominate academic culture (Clark 1983, Becher 1989). The culture of the discipline consists of a 'knowledge tradition' that includes categories of thought, a common vocabulary and related codes of conduct. The culture of the institution surrounds individual colleges and universities, generating loyalty through symbols of community and unity while permitting various subcultures to grow and flourish. Frost and Jean (1999) suggest that the culture of the professions sweeps across all disciplines and institutions, providing the basis for participation in and orientation towards a single 'community of scholars'. As Metzger (1987) has observed, many scholars have not been able to delineate clearly how these cultures clash, intersect, divide or mutually reinforce academic work (p. 2).

However, for some scholars increasing disciplinary specialization threatens to dilute the rich, local interaction that supports scholarly vitality. As the knowledge enterprise becomes increasingly complex, interdisciplinary research and learning appears to be gaining greater acceptance. It can be argued that the modern mind divides, specializes and thinks in categories, yet the Greek instinct was the opposite: to take the widest view and to see things in a more organic whole. Snow (1989) observed that the intellectual life of the West was being increasingly split, with literary intellectuals at one pole and physical scientists at the other. As a consequence, the West has lost even a pretence of common culture. This cultural divide, in Snow's view, entails serious consequences for our creative, intellectual and everyday life. These days, most of us no longer think it possible to become a Renaissance scholar, a Leonardo da Vinci. Gradually during the nineteenth century, the ideal of the unity of knowledge – that a genuine scholar ought to be familiar with the sum total of humanity's intellectual and artistic output – gave way to specialization. Humanity's ever-growing store of knowledge and the fact that each person is bestowed with a unique set of aptitudes, left most scholars and artists stranded in ever-shrinking islands of competence (Cummings 1989).

Yet, irrespective of these early suggestions that specialization and disciplinary divides are not in the best interest of learning and scholarship, there has been an increase in specialization in one form or another in higher education, despite the recent resurgence of terms such as 'interdisciplinary', 'multidisciplinary' and 'interprofessional'. In many universities across the world, the isolated individual star scholar still reigns as the desired norm (Bellah 1996, Geiger 1993). Frost and Jean (1999) argue that because research universities serve a dual purpose – of sponsored research and liberal teaching – they are susceptible to tensions that occur between specialized knowledge production and maintaining intellectual community. For some, disciplinary specialization can dampen the sense of shared purpose idealized by John Henry Newman's vision of a university experience being through 'familiar discourse'. Barnett (1994) takes this point further by suggesting that academics seem to experience a diminished sense of intellectual community in two distinct but interrelated ways. The first involves the decline of academic contact across disciplines at a local institution. The second concerns the fragmentation of communication accompanying disciplinary specialization. Communication between academics, schools, faculties or institutions becomes ever more complex as the disciplines expand their knowledge base and the methodologies contained within them. These differences between the disciplinary cultures generally appear to coalesce around several styles of enquiry, such as realism and relativism as suggested by Becher (1987, 1995) or hard and pure as suggested by Neumann et al. (2002). Academic perceptions of disciplinary differences also reflect boundary strategies employed by academics, following Durkheim's (1912/1965) functional view of culture. Here groups of academics develop boundaries as they seek to clarify their niche in the cultural space. These boundaries serve as meaningful reference points for group members and often take the form of an ethos that is frequently tested and defended. Lamont and Fournier (1992) describe how groups use cognitive and symbolic classifications to organize themselves in patterns of hierarchy or opposition in order to maintain group identity. These cognitive and symbolic boundary mechanisms give indications as to why attitudes of hierarchy, exclusion, envy and resentment among academics about various disciplines and disciplinary groups exist and remain ingrained.

Instead of being challenged by slowly emerging knowledge, as thinkers were in the Renaissance, academics are now deluged by vast quantities of new information. To avoid drowning and in order to attain some kind of security, academics seek to come ashore (to use Cummings's metaphor) on ever-smaller islands of learning and enquiry. The result is not just what Snow suggests is 'two cultures' but a multiplicity of cultures, each staking out a territory for itself, each refusing to talk to the others, and each resisting all attempted incursion from surrounding cultures (Miles 1989: 15–16). Ruscio (1986), on the other hand, takes a more sanguine view of disciplinary style and learning:

> It has become too easy to criticize esoteric research as narrow, detached, and trivial. Such criticism lacks an appreciation for the elegant way in which fields of study merge. . . . Some links facilitate integration and thereby prevent specialization from becoming narrow-mindedness . . . We need to reconceptualize our model of disciplinary growth and specialization, adopting a more organic model that accounts for the intricate links among the many specializations. Our current mechanistic model divides disciplines into numerous blocks of specializations; it is inaccurate and misleading.
>
> (pp. 43–4)

The intellectual, social and personal price of narrow compartmentalization has been commented upon over the years (Boulding 1977, Gaff 1989, Easton 1991). As Marx (1989: 9) argues, 'recent history is filled with cautionary tales [all showing] the dangerous, sometimes fatal narrowness of policies recommended by those who possess expert knowledge. Experts prefer quantifiable variables, they tend to ignore contextual complexity, and their scope is often limited.' All too often experts forget that 'problems of society do not come in discipline-shaped blocks' (Roy 1979: 165). It is therefore necessary to consider the impact of disciplinary styles on teaching and learning and the scholarship associated with them.

## Scholarship and disciplinary styles

Mary Huber (1999) of the Carnegie Foundation puts forward three related issues concerning the role disciplines have played in shaping the work and direction of the scholarship of teaching:

1. the evolution of discourses about teaching and learning
2. how discipline styles influence the design of projects on teaching and learning
3. the nature and role of interdisciplinary exchanges.

Huber suggests that these three elements will shape, and to some extent have already shaped, work on the scholarship of teaching within the disciplines in the USA and increasingly in the UK. It was hoped that communities of scholars would engage in the scholarship of teaching through the disciplines, in part because of the importance of the disciplines to the scholar's academic identity. As Grossman, Wilson and Shulman 1989 state, 'the importance of the discipline to the scholar's academic identity and in part because teaching is not a generic technique but a process that comes out of one's view of one's field and what it means to know it deeply' (p. 35).

Despite this need to belong to, and engage with, one's own identity and one's identity within a disciplinary community, Shulman suggests that 'every faculty member in higher education belongs to both a "visible" and an "invisible" college, and one must work with both to expand the focus of journals, academic conferences, and hiring processes to give a higher profile to the scholarship of teaching on campus and beyond' (1999: 17). The aim of these statements and perceptions was and remains to bring the disciplines and their ways of working to the forefront of higher-education discourse. Shulman (1987) argues that the reason for focusing on the scholarship of teaching within the disciplines is that it deepens our understanding of teaching knowledge. Cross (1990) extends this argument by suggesting that it sharpens our focus on student learning, and broadens our definitions of academic scholarship (Boyer 1990, Glassick, Huber and Maeroff 1997), thus widening our views of the audience for teaching, to include peers as well as students (Hutchings 1996, 1998, Shulman 1997).

It is very clear from these arguments why the scholarship of teaching has begun to focus on disciplines and disciplinary approaches to learning. Yet there is still a significant reluctance by academics to separate out questions relating to subject knowledge, in which they are meant to be expert, from those relating to how the subject should be taught, whether in the interest of the students learning or from a learning perspective of academic staff themselves. Cross argues that expert research on teaching and learning will likely be discovered by scholars only when they start asking questions that such literature (educational research) may help them formulate and resolve. Requiring discipline-based academics to engage in educational research or at the very least reading and enquiring into educational issues needs a considerable change of mindset that is not essentially congruent with the demands of higher education, i.e. the development and output of high-quality research. One of the challenges still facing teaching and learning in higher education is disciplinary style. Also important here is acknowledging what Özesmi (1999: 3) argues – that 'a scholar can not imagine a new form of scholarship without any reference to the past or to the academic institutions that have existed prior to the act of thinking. Therefore in locating this new form of scholarship we inherently have to face disciplinarity itself.'

Disciplinary styles influence the way scholars approach learning and teaching just as they do their research methodology and perspectives (Marcus 1998). A disciplinary style comprises, at its core, what Schwab so elegantly distinguished as 'substantive and syntactic structures: the "conceptions that guide enquiry" and the "pathways of enquiry" [scholars] use, what they mean by verified knowledge and how they go about verification' (1964: 25, 21). What Schwab is intimating is that disciplinary style influences the problems academics choose to engage with, the methods used to explore the problems and the nature of the arguments that develop from those explorations. This perspective reinforces Huber's (1999) argument that a majority of academics in most disciplines work with traditional ways of teaching and learning and are relatively unaware of or indifferent to the communities of educational researchers and reformers. It is interesting to note the research concerning the different behaviours shown by academic staff in respect of teaching when viewed against their disciplinary backgrounds. Biglan (1973b), Clark (1987), Smeby (1996) and most recently Neumann et al. (2002) have shown how academics in the hard pure fields tune in with the competitive nature of the working environment and manifest a strong commitment to research and a correspondingly weaker one to teaching. This is not surprising when we consider Özesmi's research on disciplinarity and scholars, which found that 'scholarship and disciplines have been under the support, control, and exploitation of the very structures that are part of social dementia' (p. 3).

## The issue of teaching and learning within the disciplines

Why is it that within higher education the ideas of the disciplines dominate the discussions relating to teaching and learning? Contextually, it is understandable why academics need to refer back to their own discipline as a source of security, but what happens when they come out of this safe environment and decide to explore the parameters of their discipline within the learning environment? Palmer (1998) suggests that 'by understanding our fear, we could overcome the structures of disconnection with power of self-knowledge' (p. 37).

What is the fear that keeps academics so closely tied to their disciplines? Again, as Palmer suggests, the answer seems obvious: it is a fear of 'losing my job or my image or my status if I do not pay homage to institutional powers' (p. 37). However, this perspective does not adequately explain the depth of the issue. Palmer suggests that academics 'collaborate with the structures of separation because they promise to protect us against one of the deepest fears at the heart of being human – the fear of having a live encounter with alien "otherness", whether the other is a student, a colleague, a subject, or a self-dissenting voice within'. Palmer further argues that the reason why there is such anxiety within the community is because:

> We fear encounters in which the other is free to be itself, to speak its own truth, to tell us what we may not wish to hear. We want encounters on our own terms, so that we can control their outcomes, so that they will not threaten our view of world and self. Academic institutions offer myriad ways to protect ourselves from the threat of a live encounter. To avoid live encounters, students can hide behind their notebooks and their silence. To avoid a live encounter with students, teachers can hide behind their podiums, their credentials, and their power. To avoid a live encounter with one another, faculty can hide behind their academic specialties. To avoid a live encounter with subjects of study, teachers and students alike can hide behind the pretence of objectivity. . . . To avoid a live encounter with ourselves, we can learn the art of self-alienation, of living a divided life.
>
> (Palmer 1998: 37)

These comments shed light on the pressure within academic life to be successful and remain in good standing within one's particular discipline or allegiances. Palmer identifies key aspects of the academic's life in terms of the power of belonging to a discipline or allegiance, plus the need to engage with students, learning, teaching and one's own beliefs and values. Within this context it is not surprising that disciplines and discipline approaches to scholarship remain strong, as, consequently, does the belief that disciplines also hold the key to teaching and learning. Research has shown that although academics emphasize the need to understand the various dimensions in the culture of the academy that shape academic attitudes and behaviours, often within academic life, intellectual, affective and symbolic meanings coalesce around various points of convergence and tension specific to their territory and discipline (Astin 1990, Dill 1991, Peterson and Spencer 1990, Tierney and Rhoads 1994). Such affective and symbolic bonds among academics often underlie such behaviour, despite elaborate pretensions to the contrary (Clark 1983: 74). It is therefore possible to see how, Palmer describes, fear significantly influences academic engagement in the higher-education community. This is directly reflected in the nature of scholarship, teaching and learning.

Breaking down the notion of fear or the idea of a live encounter is essential to understanding why academics inhabit their space in the way that they do. Palmer (1998) suggests that the fear of a live encounter is actually a sequence of fears that begins with a fear of diversity. He argues, 'as long as we inhabit a universe made homogeneous by our refusal to admit otherness, we can maintain the illusion that we possess the truth about ourselves and the world – after all, there is no "other" to challenge us! But as soon as we admit pluralism, we are forced to admit that ours is not the only standpoint, the only experience, the only way, and the truths we have built our lives on begin to feel fragile' (p. 38). The point here is that Palmer is not referring merely to diversity of students but to the whole academic way of life. Disciplines are not the only way to consider issues, nor are they the only way to engage with scholarship, learning and teaching. It is the embracing of diverse ways of considering truths that is important to moving a learning community forward. Understanding different ways of thinking and behaving requires academics to consider different mindsets, and this in itself causes the academic community a problem.

In most instances academic communities work in competition with each other, whether with respect to research grants, teaching excellence or league tables. Most activities can be perceived as being a contest from which an individual, a team or a university emerges victorious while the others feel rejected or demoralized. As a consequence of these competitive, conflict-ridden engagements, many academics shun, evade or do not engage with such high-profile public activities, as they see the differences to be dangerous and not part of their academic world. As a result there is a tendency for academics and the academic community to keep these views to themselves, only to find them grow stronger, more diverse and fragmented.

Why should this be the case, when academics are generally free-thinking autonomous individuals? Here again Palmer helps to take the argument forward by suggesting that 'peeling back the fear of conflict is actually about a fear of losing one's identity' (1998: 45). Individual academics are very deeply associated with their discipline or subject base; their ideas, values and beliefs are part of their being. Hence in a competitive encounter, the individual or team may risk losing more than the debate, grant tender or reputation for scholar-ship; they risk losing their sense of self. Within disciplines themselves, academics are vulnerable to challenges to their work from other academics. This is a threatening situation, especially to those in powerful positions and those starting out on their academic careers. Although the threats to the concept of self may be different, they are equally intimidating. Power in academia is built around disciplines and power struggles take place within and around these bodies of knowledge. As Bourdieu (1988) would argue, the power of the *habitus* is considerable.

These are persuasive arguments for understanding the power of a discipline base. Yet fear can also be a good thing; it can be trans-formative, helping individuals to change and learn to survive in differing conditions and situations. These notions of fear are further developed in Chapter 7 in relation to risk. However, the 'fear factor' is an interesting concept in terms of positive developments within discipline boundaries. A fear that one is teaching poorly or producing weak scholarship may not be a sign of weakness but evidence that the individual or team cares about the activities that they are engaged in. For example, the fear of teaching a topic that may create a controversial or difficult learning situation within a classroom may not be a warning not to engage with that activity but a signal that the topic needs to be addressed, sensitively and possibly from a variety of perspectives not considered previously. Insight from other disciplines may be required to give constructive direction as to how such topics may be taught and engaged with. Crossing these boundaries in this way is still not the norm in higher education. It therefore becomes imperative for those in the higher-education community to be capable of understanding the need to cross boundaries, as well as understanding the fears associated with crossing boundaries. Understanding fears and risks is key to engaging academics from across the disciplines. As Palmer states, 'the fear that makes people "porous" to real learning is a healthy fear that enhances education' (1998: 51). But as academics within an academic community we must understand and engage with these fears if we are to learn from them. Maybe when academics understand how and where to cross the boundaries real learning will occur. Then learning and scholarship might be challenged.

# Ways of knowing

Research surrounding the disciplines identifies that each discipline claims to have its own mode of learning (Huber 1999, Neumann et al. 2002). Such dominant modes of learning can be assumed to stem from two fundamental questions: how do academics know what they know within their discipline and by what warrant can they call that knowledge true? The answers to these questions are often tacit and sometimes unconscious, but most often they are communicated in the way academics teach and learn. However, essential to understanding disciplinary concepts is the ability to think critically about the nature of knowledge and the ways in which knowledge is produced and validated, as well as having an awareness of the epistemological and value-based commitments that are present in all knowledge claims. Academics in particular should be sensitive to the ways in which these commitments vary between different disciplines. This is most prevalent in subjects that consider themselves interdisciplinary. Jones et al. (1999) argue that there is no single universally accepted theory concerning the production of knowledge, including scientific knowledge. They suggest that academics have developed a wide range of more or less distinct theories, each with an epistemological approach, where epistemology is taken to be a branch of philosophy concerned with theories of knowledge, or theories of how we can know about the world.

Much of Anglo-American philosophy has been concerned with developing what can be termed *realist* approaches to epistemology. Although these can be subdivided into various categories, a common feature is that they allow for the possibility of purely objective knowledge; that is, knowledge of external reality which is independent of the subject and her/his historical cultural context. This mode of knowing has been called *objectivism*, as it suggests that something can be achieved by disconnecting ourselves, physically and emotionally, from the thing we want to know. Objectivism can be thought of as distancing the individual from something, which thus becomes an object; when it becomes an object, it no longer has life; when it is lifeless, it cannot touch or transform us, so knowledge of the thing remains pure (Palmer 1998). When related to teaching, learning and scholarship, this notion of objectivism is interesting. Although possibly used subconsciously by academics, could it be that it often forms the basis for lack of real engagement and understanding of concepts such as teaching and learning? Emotional involvement in either could cause the 'fear factor' to emerge. Isolation and objective consideration of teaching and learning is by far the easier option, particularly when framed through an individual's discipline base.

The learning, teaching and scholarship experience in higher education is influenced by a wide range of values which may relate to the academic community as a whole, to specific discipline-based teams or the individual. These values may be explicit and form the foundations for teaching, learning and scholarship within the institution, team or individual. As research has shown, these values and dominant ways of knowing are key to disciplines retaining their individual and strong frames of reference. Reybold (2001, 2003) has argued that the act of knowing constitutes identity, thus connecting identity to epistemological perspectives.

Connecting epistemological perspectives to identity and frames of reference of individuals highlights again academics' need to work within disciplines and 'zones of comfort'. It also can explain why learning, teaching and scholarship are so closely tied to individuals' frames of reference. This is further reinforced when Lave and Wenger's (1991) concepts of situated learning and legitimate peripheral participation are used as a framework for understanding how learning and experience 'are in constant interaction – indeed are mutually constitutive' (p. 52). Learning, they argue, needs to be defined more broadly than accumulation of new knowledge; learning 'implies becoming a full participant, a member, a kind of person' (p. 53) within a community of practice. In the case of becoming a department member the academic has to practise as others do within that community, whether in terms of teaching, learning or scholarship. The concept of legitimate peripheral participation supports the concept of an emergent professional identity during the academic's experience within a set discipline. As Rogoff (1984) argued, 'context is an integral aspect of cognitive events, not a nuisance variable' (p. 3). However, as Reybold (2003) argues, participative or situated learning is broader than literal and physical interactions with others. On the other hand, Cobbs and Bowers (1999) remind us that individual actions involve 'an encompassing system of social practices' which constitutes learning about and participation in those social practices (p. 5). The construction of practitioner identity, in this case the academic within a set discipline, is both social and developmental, an 'evolving form of membership' in a community of practice (Lave and Wenger 1991: 5). Understanding what it means to be a member of a department/discipline is a key aspect of determining the issues related to teaching and learning within the disciplines. Research shows that emphasis on traditional academic values within academic communities helps to strengthen and support academic vitality and scholarly commitment (Bland and Schmitz 1990), and therefore perpetuate the boundaries of separation. If this approach is taken to its limits it could be argued that 'universities today are a collection of disciplines and sub-disciplines, each pursuing their own kinds of knowledge, carelessly assuming that some invisible hand of wisdom will shape the whole into intelligible patterns' (Frost and Jean 1999: 125).

However, as successful as the specialized, disciplinary approach to knowledge, scholarship, teaching and learning has been, and as essential as it may continue to be in higher education, it is not sufficient to address the ever-increasing complexities of knowledge creation and proliferation.

## Disciplines, power, students' learning and curriculum

Influential in this area has been the work of Smart et al. (2000); the case they put forward is that there has been very little common research connecting those who study academic communities and academic disciplines, and those who study change among students over the course of their experience in higher education. In their book *Academic Disciplines*, Smart et al. discuss the lack of connection between the research and the practicalities within the academy. What is interesting for the present discussion here in relation to the disciplines and scholarship is that Smart et al. suggest that the differences in disciplinary cultures have a significant influence on students and their future perceptions of and attitudes to scholarship and learning. The theoretical framework of the research is Holland's theory, which is based on the foundation that behaviour is basically the interaction between individuals and their environment, that individuals have identifiable personality types, and that individuals flourish in environments compatible with those personalities. A particularly interesting finding has been that students choose academic environments compatible with their personality types; that faculty reinforce and reward behaviours consistent with their environmental types, to which student behaviour and attitudes respond over time; and that the people who flourish in these environments are consistent in terms of personality types.

The major significance of these findings for higher education is that students who have selected disciplinary foci consistent with their personality types make the most substantial moves towards congruence with the values and intellectual frameworks of their disciplines. Those who have studied against type move towards the pure characteristics, but to a lesser degree. These patterns hold for both 'primary' recruits to a discipline (those who choose a field and stay with it over a three- to four-year period) and 'secondary' recruits (those who change their courses). It could be argued that these findings reflect common sense and only what might be expected from students in higher education. However, the research goes further, to suggest that moves towards particular behaviours which are reinforced by 'faculty' behaviour; and expectations can and do influence students' learning and future development within the given discipline or outside it. Smart et al. suggest that more specific attention be given to the acculturation and behaviours that are shaped and reinforced by academic departments. How might such behaviour and approaches to learning, teaching and scholarship within the disciplines affect student and academic engagement? If such reinforcement of behaviour exists and shapes student development then it is possible to ask the question 'What effect might this have on curricula and learning?'

Tradition is a key aspect of any discipline and traditional courses by their very nature emphasize topics over process. Curriculum is often interpreted as course structure and course content, and little attention is paid to pedagogical activities. Educational goals are coloured by disciplinary philosophy and are frequently recorded as having been achieved when students give correct answers, which may require not only accurate discipline knowledge, but most importantly accurate discipline-based behavioural responses. Training students within the disciplines becomes a set of behaviours that requires students to answer questions correctly, but also to seek to ask the questions in the correct way, again reinforcing discipline expectations. Frequently within this cycle of development and learning, the role of learning and the experience of learning are grossly underestimated. Learning is frequently interpreted as knowledge acquisition rather than knowledge construction. Most disciplinary courses aim to impart a predefined and fixed amount of established knowledge, concepts and skills, often ignoring the need for the student to explore, imagine and be creative. 'This traditional approach is a great mismatch for self-directed and discovery-orientated learners. Indeed, repeated learning experience in this format often makes many creative and discovery-orientated students uninterested in the course work or results in forced and frustrating conversions of many potentially creative students into dependent and passive learners' (Goel 2004: 1).

Mounting evidence indicates that the sources of influence on students' learning are as varied and interconnected as the ways students learn (Pascarella and Terenzini 1991). For example, not only are gains in critical thinking ability accompanied by changes in students' self-identities, self-esteem and an array of attitudes and values, but also the sources of influence on the development of critical thinking are themselves varied and interrelated (Terenzini et al. 1994, 1995). Such views of learning demand consideration of multiple educational outcomes that include complex cognitive skills, and an ability to apply knowledge to practical problems. Recognizing that students are active participants, not passive recipients, in the learning process is a central component whatever the discipline or area of learning. However, teaching students actively to develop knowledge, to evaluate information and evidence, and make informed decisions requires modelling processes that engage students in practising such skills and acknowledging both student and teacher subjectivity. As Palmer (1998) argues, 'we bring ourselves to the teaching process, just as our students bring themselves to the learning process'; he notes that one of the difficult truths about teaching is that it 'will never take unless it connects with the inward, living core of our students' lives' (p. 20). If Palmer's views are to be taken seriously as well as the research of Smart (2000), curricula and teaching methods have to be reconsidered from a learning perspective by all disciplines. However, curricula, research programmes and teaching methods are subjects of continual power struggles within the disciplines because they constitute the use of knowledge most directly of interest to academics. Courses can focus on academic issues or on broad applications; they can sample a range of views or be very partisan. So why do academics introduce certain aspects or content to their courses and not others? Martin (1998: 3) suggests that there are a variety of reasons, but that it is predominantly because specific content is used by academics to 'stake out a domain of expertise and to increase individual status as a critical intellectual'. In many ways a more fundamental challenge to the academic power structures is introducing new teaching methodologies, which give students more control over their learning. The most powerful academic staff usually have an interest in ensuring that teaching is orientated primarily to the discipline, not the students. The reason for this is that academic power is based on control over knowledge and core areas of the discipline, thus ensuring that the power base of the subject is continued through the student-learning environment. Academics who promote alternative methodologies, which are student orientated and embrace the mutual interaction of students' and teachers' thinking and learning, are essentially seen as linking with their students and not the discipline, and as a consequence are perceived as less discipline biased within the power structures (Baxter and Terenzini 2002).

Teachers and students learning together implies transforming assumptions about instructional effectiveness, the role of teaching in faculty life, and the role of educator in student affairs (Baxter and Terenzini 2002). This transformation has to be both discipline based and generic within the academy. Understanding learning situations and how individuals learn should be a starting point for the disciplines and the academic community as a whole. Research is increasingly contributing to our understanding of how students and individuals learn. Research demonstrates how complex the learning process is and that academics need time and space to learn about learning. Shulman (1993) suggests that 'teaching must become community property' and academics need to be supported in the endeavours of making teaching and learning public. To facilitate such developments Baxter and Terenzini (2002) argue that the task of transforming assumptions about students' role in the campus community has to be addressed by academics. Just as new forms of pedagogy call for partnerships with learners, partnerships within educational communities will also be needed (p. 8). The implication here is that, whereas in the past discipline-based staff and the academic community within disciplines were solely responsible for educational practice, a more joint perspective will be needed in the future – one that takes account of past experience and expertise of both the students and staff. Intellectual curiosity belongs to all who wish to learn.

## Disciplinary power, barriers to change

The different ways in which the disciplines interpret the very nature of their worlds inhibit universities from implementing an integrated, interdisciplinary approach to learning. To academics, the disciplines seem a self-evident way of dividing and organizing knowledge. Disciplinary divisions are more entrenched in higher education than any other aspect of learning and development, and the entrenchment is connected to the power disciplines hold within the academic structures. These notions of disciplinary power do not contribute towards understanding learning and the need to conceptualize learning within a scholarly framework. Appreciating that knowledge creation is key to scholarly activity does not necessitate a disciplinary approach.

The idea of the social construction of knowledge gives a vital clue to understanding the dynamics of the disciplines and the power base that they hold within the academic community. Martin (1998) suggests that the disciplines are not based on inherent characteristics of knowledge or reality. Rather, the disciplines can best be understood as resulting from divisions of knowledge which are useful for the purposes of groups of people: academics, professionals, capitalists and state bureaucrats. The development and maintenance of a body of knowledge as a discipline involves a continual power struggle. Those who control teaching and research in a discipline use that control to expand their own empires or to ward off threats. The existing organization of knowledge is hard to change. People's careers are built on it, and their perceptions grow out of it. So the past history of disciplines is one of the key factors in their continuing development (Ch. 4 p. 1). Martin continues his argument by suggesting that:

> as academia is built around disciplines, power struggles take place within and around these bodies of knowledge. Powerful figures in a discipline usually rise to their positions by pursuing research of a conventional kind, typically along a narrow specialisation without much deviation. By becoming the moguls of a thin slice of knowledge, the rising stars of the discipline ward off challenges and stake claims for more influence and control.
>
> (Ch. 4 p. 4)

Alternatively, academic power struggles within disciplines can be framed around closure, i.e. the cutting off of a 'fringe' perspective or individuals by demanding adherence to a particular core of knowledge. What is significant here is that a consequence of these types of division of knowledge into disciplines is the squeezing out of anyone or any group that does not fit within the usual frameworks. Those whose scholarship cuts across the disciplines or who are tied to powerless groups are found to flounder and struggle. Areas that fall outside the disciplines provide fewer career opportunities and lack the status of pure disciplinary work. Nowhere is this more evident than in discipline-based educational research.

Against this backdrop it is possible to see why change in attitudes to learning is difficult. For academics within disciplines to become partners in a shared common understanding of learning will require them to consider how their discipline is identified within a framework of learning, and how the academic community responds to and understands it. Understanding learning and the need to recognize learning within a scholarly framework does not necessitate a lessening of power for disciplines, but does require them to see future power struggles within the boundary of learning. The disciplinary constraints found within the academy need to be reconsidered, for the barriers they construct to ensure their continuation could ultimately conspire to be their downfall. As Einstein so eloquently stated, 'imagination is more important than knowledge'.

*Chapter 6*

# An international perspective: the implications of scholarship for professionalism

*Simon Lygo-Baker*

> A multitude of men are made one person, when they are by one man, or
> one person represented; so that it be done with the consent of everyone of
> that multitude in particular.
>
> (Hobbes)

Chapter 5 introduced some of the debates surrounding the meaning
ascribed to the scholarship of teaching and argued that the term is
currently being used in the UK to raise the status of those promoting
it. The chapter also suggested that the scholarship of teaching could be
utilized more effectively by the academic community as a mechanism
to explore teaching and learning and provide greater understanding
of the interrelationship between the two. Changing the emphasis
so that the scholarship of teaching is utilized productively within
the higher-education environment means enhancing the understanding of learning in the academic community and reconceptualizing
scholarship in the way that was argued for in Chapter 3.

The primary focus of scholarship in higher education originated
as teaching. In the nineteenth century the notion of 'research' entered
the definitions at universities such as Oxford and Cambridge which
argued that they were strongholds of testing truth and expanding
knowledge and then disseminating this through teaching. As has
been expanded on in earlier chapters, scholarship is now explained
and conceptualized almost exclusively in terms of discovery and
research. This chapter examines the notion of professionalism and its

relationship with the scholarship of teaching to consider how far the shift from scholarship being defined by research to the exclusion of teaching has continued. The promotion of the scholarship of teaching may appear to redress the balance but an examination of the notion of professionalism questions the implications and motives behind the advancement of the concept.

Evidence is then drawn from the USA, the UK and Australia concerning the ways in which the higher-education community has embraced the concept of the scholarship of teaching. Examination of this evidence suggests that the different contexts may bring different interpretations and understandings of the concept. Within each context the question is raised as to who defines and gives meaning to the scholarship of teaching: academics, policy makers or a combination of both.

Change has become a constant for those in any occupation in the twenty-first century. For those in the higher-education community there has been a particular need to respond to the discourses of 'marketisation and globalisation' (Santoro 2003), which have brought with them a series of significant and destabilizing challenges. Nixon et al. (2001) note that the challenges have threatened the structures, traditions and public view of the higher-education landscape and thus have altered the status quo for those working within it and those who impact on it, such as government. The outlook remains uncertain, with further challenges ahead in the form of a continued expansion in student numbers, real-terms resource depletion and changes to the traditional work of the academic; all of which provide a catalyst for a reinterpretation of the role of a scholar. In response to such a major series of challenges the traditional identity of the academic has come under increasing pressure to adapt, as discussed in Chapter 4. Breakwell (1986) suggests that when 'communities' find themselves threatened they develop coping strategies. As Chapter 5 illustrated, the development of the notion of the scholarship of teaching has been based around a misguided interpretation of the term. The academic community may have been tempted to accept the interpretation offered in order to cope with increasing change. The notion of the scholarship of teaching may also appeal to those in academic roles because it suggests a professional status. As the 'knowledge' of an academic becomes increasingly challenged by a more questioning public, the scholarship of teaching provides another coping strategy with which to defend the legitimacy of an academic's professional knowledge.

# The risk society and the impact on values

Beck (1992) and Bauman (1999) have both suggested that in the twentieth century society became uncertain of its direction as it lurched from one crisis to the next. The modernist state found itself increasingly unable to provide systems of prediction and therefore control. As a result, they argue, society has moved into a postmodern state that is highly unstable. Giddens (1999) develops this argument, suggesting that in response to this instability the postmodern state has evolved a 'manufactured risk'. The difficulty for individuals within this state is explained when we consider the suggestion made by experiential learning theorists. They argue that individuals use previous under-standing to help explain a new situation. This gives meaning to the experience and assists people to act instinctively. However, a difficulty with this approach appears when past knowledge and understanding are unable to relate easily to the present situation. The previous learning fails to cope with the new information and we become aware that we no longer know how to act: a 'disjuncture' occurs (Jarvis 1995). The incidence of disjuncture in society and particularly in higher education is increasing. Without previous experience to help interpret the information and enable adequate predictions to be made, Giddens argues that we turn to our value structures.

These value structures help us to describe the situation and provide a way forward through the crises as they are identified. The rapidity and regularity of change that is now part of the postmodern state can be seen to have impacted within the higher-education landscape, where regular structural changes broadly fit with the discourse of 'marketization' (Adams 1998, Mawditt 1998, Santoro 2003). Added to this, Archer (1984) has argued that the current systems that have emerged have done so from very complex structures and cultures. She reinforces Giddens's views by arguing that it is values that play an important role in enabling practitioners to maintain a sense of their role in higher education. There are, however, difficulties for individuals within this environment. According to Sullivan (2003), uncertainty and disjuncture are increased by the postmodern university, which 'screens out' the individual and their experiences and thus overlooks important factors in understanding scholarship. Individual passions, prejudices, commitments, beliefs and values are constrained and not acknowledged within the definitions and meanings offered.

As higher education has faced these new and increasingly complex challenges, the values displayed and their public interaction have significantly increased. Acknowledging that the challenges created by and in the postmodern state have impacted upon these values is very important because it is these values that provide a view of the identity of those within the community and help define what it is to be a professional member of it. In trying to respond to the contestability of the frameworks (Barnett 2000) within which academics are now working, shared values drawn up 'corporately' offer potential stability and common ground. Santoro suggests that this has occurred in the academic community and that academics have sought to use these values to maintain and affirm their professional status. Stilwell (2003) argues that the increased emphasis on commercial approaches in higher education has challenged any conventional notions of professionalism based around individual autonomy. The challenge, according to Mawditt (1998: 323), is one born out of a 'necessity to become more business minded' and is at odds with the individual values that many hold. A dilemma is therefore created for academics: either acknowledge that change is having an impact and accept the values that are redrawn in line with the new context; or reject the change and retain values that may hold within some areas of the academic community but that may have little support outside it and may not fit the institutional profile. Sullivan argues that this process results in a denial of our individual fundamental understandings and interpretations that should play a part in understanding scholarship.

The result? The academic community is faced with fragmentation at a time when it needs to adjust to radical and widespread change. By holding on to the old individual values academics may leave themselves vulnerable and unable to respond to the changes taking place. Accepting new values may appear to offer the academic the opportunity to understand their actions and predict the impact of these actions in the future. According to Bauman (1999) the likelihood is that faced with this choice the majority will opt for an adoption of the new reconstructed values. Reflecting the much earlier philosophy of Jeremy Bentham and his notion of the Panopticon, Bauman argues that individuals are happy to concede authority, as they prefer a controlled environment which suggests a return to the state where prediction of outcomes can be made. When uncertainty does occur, individuals come together in 'communities' to overcome their fears, and each community attempts to appear stronger than another. Could the growing interest in the scholarship of teaching represent the instigation of just such a created community, suggesting as it has a new professional set of standards for teaching and learning in higher education and providing as it does some stable ground and a response to disjuncture?

# Professionalism and scholarship

Nixon (2001: 178) argues that what is needed is 'a reorientation of professional values and practices such that academic workers "use" their academic freedom as *freedom for all'*. In doing so he echoes the traditional view that Aristotle proposed, whereby individuals have a moral obligation not to desert humanity when they reach understanding but rather to serve it. A realization of the connection between the world that the academic inhabits and the world outside is achieved through scholarship. This connection is expedited through research or teaching. The danger is that within the changing landscape in which the university functions, where there is a growing emphasis on quality control, increased regulation and the development of comparative standards, the professional values developed are based not on those of the individual academic in relation to scholarship but on some 'common' notion of professionalism drawn from a wider base. The regulation and the standards that accompany this notion of professionalism dilute and manipulate the connections and the values on which the individual draws. As a result, the meaning of scholarship becomes obscured behind a smoke screen called 'professionalism'. Whilst there is clearly a close relationship between the notion of the scholarship of teaching and notions of professionalism (Healey 2003, quoting Baume 1999), the blurring of the boundary between the two may be something that is tacitly acknowledged by some and wilfully ignored by others. The danger is that the values that relate to being an academic and engaged with the scholarship of teaching are formulated and manipulated by those outside the profession in the name of professionalism. The reorientation Nixon calls for is against a set of professional values that the academic community has not defined. The freedom of the academic becomes limited and, by association, in reality so does the freedom of the student. Curricula become constrained, calls for consistent university approaches are answered and standards and criteria multiply. Those within the academy, tired of constant change, uncertain of their future, accept an apparent common value as part of their coping strategy. According to a recent multi-agency document in the UK, 'Professionalism is commonly understood as an individual's adherence to a set of standards, code of conduct or collection of qualities that characterise accepted practice within a particular area of activity' (Universities UK, 2004). The notion of standards replaces values and is indicative of the greater administrative emphasis that is occurring with the aim of enabling measurement and greater prediction of outcomes.

The challenge to academic freedom can be recognized and interpreted through an examination of society's expectations about occupational groups, which have grown. The label 'professional', while suggesting credibility, now also brings with it the implication of increased scrutiny. Greater awareness and consciousness about professional groups has led to the 'untouchables' becoming increasingly exposed to the public. This in turn has raised expectations and increased accountability. Teaching at all levels has become more openly scrutinized and academics are being encouraged to develop a more professionalized interest in the development of their teaching and learning. This in turn has led those in higher education to engage in more critical self-reflection and the development of quality assurance measures in the name of enhancing educational services (Farrugia 1996). Whilst this may undoubtedly have positive effects, especially if the former predominates, there is a danger that the values that have helped to create an identity over many years will be reinterpreted or replaced with more temporary, reactive values that respond to a different agenda – that of quality assurance. Barnett (1994) has therefore questioned whether the notion of professionalism in teaching is actually relevant or desirable when in reality the process has been described as 'deprofessionalizing' the higher-education staff. The blame for this is levelled at the quality assurance agenda becoming too predominant, thus restricting innovation and discovery, which in turn restricts the traditional meaning and understanding of scholarship.

Interestingly, much of the argument presented thus far has suggested that the individual is no longer at the centre of the debate. According to Friedson (1994) autonomy is the central component of professionalism. A profession needs to have the right to control its own work and determine who can do the work and how it should be undertaken. Evidence from previous chapters has suggested that this autonomy has been restricted and is no longer applied to the individual academic. An examination of Downie's (1990) six characteristics of a professional may illuminate how and where the autonomy has been restricted.

1. *Having a skill or expertise drawn from a broad knowledge base.* As argued in Chapter 4, academics have taken refuge on ever-smaller islands of learning or enquiry. Although the potential knowledge base has increased rapidly, many have found this unsettling, as the ability to predict future outcomes has decreased. The traditional role of the academic has therefore increasingly become challenged. Can an academic really keep up to date with so much information?

2. *Providing a service based on a special relationship with those whom s/he serves. The relationship is based upon fairness, honesty and a bond based on ethical and legal rights and duties authorized by the professional institution and legalized by public esteem.* The relationship between the academic and the community that he or she serves has clearly become more complex, since that community is now less static and increasingly diverse and demanding. Again the traditional role of the academic has become increasingly challenged. The institution within which the academic works has a greater influence and impact on the relationship between the academic and the community.

3. *Achieving public recognition as having the authority to speak on broad matters that go beyond service to specific clients.* The authority of academics to speak on issues related to their disciplines remains but is now questioned more openly. The modern academic is likely to find his or her views open to greater scrutiny and there are competing interests that engage in these discussions, such as corporate groups.

4. *Being independent of the influence of the state or commercial aspects.* Following on from the point above, the academic community often now finds itself in partnership with both the state and commercial interests. As a result, the ability of the academic community to retain independence is questionable. The development of programmes is now often at the behest and according to the requirements of a professional body or organization.

5. *Having been educated rather than trained and therefore having a wider cognitive perspective that continues to develop his/her knowledge and skills within a framework of values.* At first there may appear little difficulty over this aspect of the definition. Academics are expected to be educated in their discipline and through their continuing research to extend this over time. The boundary between education and training becomes less obvious when we consider teaching. Many academics have received little or no education or training on the complex relationship between teaching and learning. Many of the current initiatives in the higher-education sector to enhance the teaching and learning of academics would struggle to convince close scrutiny that they go beyond providing training 'tips'. To ensure that academics examine their values in relation to teaching requires education and engagement with the theories relating to learning.

6. *Having legitimized authority and credibility in the eyes of the general public.* The authority of academics has increasingly been questioned, as

indeed has that of many public professionals, such as doctors. Legitimized authority may be drawn from the institution or a professional body but, as stated in the fourth point above, this may then have an impact on the values of the individual and therefore affect his or her independence.

When the chief executive of the Quality Assurance Agency in the UK argued for 'professionalism' to be ascribed more to institutions than to individuals (Nixon et al. 2001), he underlined the trend to remove individual autonomy and replace it with some shared notion of professionalism defined by common values. The crucial question is where the values that form this professionalism stem from. Are they, or indeed should they be, from the individuals within higher education or from those outside? Nixon et al. argue that whilst professionalism is a complex interrelation of values, these should stem from the individual. Whatever the institution stands for, the individual has to rely upon his or her own values drawn from his or her own practice. As discussed in Chapter 3, the difficulty is that the development of these values is extremely complex. Although an individual draws these values from his or her own discipline, there is a range of other influences that need to be considered. Scholarly activity is demonstrated by an individual in and out of a range of different social habitats, and as Sullivan (2003: 134) suggests, our 'intellectual acts are inextricably embedded in and influenced by the life that accompanies them'.

## A 'bottom-up' approach

Much of the discussion about the scholarship of teaching considered thus far has been at a macro level and appears bound by institution and political views. It is important to examine any evidence that may challenge this view and suggest that the scholarship of teaching is also influenced by individuals and individual disciplines' approaches. According to Healey (2003) the American Association for Higher Education (AAHE) has worked to try and bring a subject perspective to the debate over the scholarship of teaching in the US. The Carnegie Foundation also helps to bring together scholars from a variety of disciplines to further discussions. In Australia the Committee for the Advancement of Teaching and Learning in Higher Education (CATLHE) has worked to promote teaching and learning through disciplines. In the UK there has been a series of initiatives aimed at examining and developing scholarly activity, such as the Fund for the Development of Teaching and Learning (FDTL) and most recently the Centres for Excellence in Teaching and Learning (CETL). The aim of the CETL initiative is to:

> recognise, celebrate and promote excellence by rewarding teachers who have made a demonstrable impact on student learning and who enthuse, motivate and influence others to do the same. We envisage that CETLs will sustain and stimulate further excellent practice through teaching that is informed by scholarly reflection.
>
> (HEFCE 2004: 3)

Lueddeke (2003) argues that if we are to provide a plausible conceptualization of the scholarship of teaching we need to acknowledge rather than exclude the influence of individual disciplines. Lueddeke's own research suggests that it is the discipline that one belongs to and how the individual conceptualizes teaching that are crucial variables. His findings indicate that understanding and developing teaching scholarship requires a complex 'integration between rational, political, social interaction and human problem-solving processes' (p. 223). The values and beliefs within the discipline influence and shape how individuals see their world. A problem that Huber (1999) takes up from this is that as disciplines place such different values upon what the scholarship of teaching is, the final outcome may prove to be a serious lack of consensus. This creates a challenge and Huber asks whether it is possible to reconceptualize scholarship so that it is meaningful to all disciplines without making one approach to it appear to be more privileged. This enterprise is further complicated in the postmodern era by the fact that boundaries are constantly blurred and shifting between disciplines. As Henkel (2000) found, teaching identities are very much shaped by the context. This reflects the work of McInnis (1993), who suggested that the institution had a key part to play, along with the discipline and team, in the development of individual values.

Menand (1996) has warned that the traditional view of relating or belonging to a discipline is breaking down and being replaced by a sense of relating to an institution. In other words, the main social *habitus* has shifted from the discipline to the institution (see Figure 6.1). Individuals therefore no longer set their values according to their discipline but relate them to the context of the institution within which they work. Menand argues that as a consequence of these

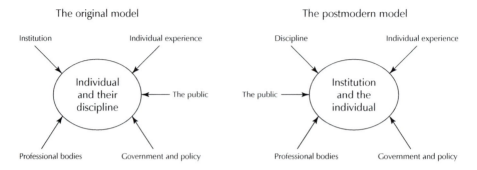

*Figure 6.1* Academics and their sense of belonging

administrative developments the differences between universities are now substantial. Interestingly, Nixon (2001) points out that as a result of these changes within the postmodern world, academic freedom no longer originates from the traditional disciplinary difference. It now develops from institutional difference and this is where the values are drawn from. He reiterates, however, that the individual should still draw upon these values.

The difficulty for academic freedom and the understanding of the scholarship of teaching is that even if the individual still retains autonomy (and this is questionable), the context within which this occurs has changed. Whereas individuals were traditionally able to undertake an exploration of their values without external pressure and in line with their discipline and then consider how these might fit across academia, the postmodern state has altered the context. As a result academics have become increasingly required to develop their values against an administrative set of criteria, developed by external groups or interests, with less focus upon the discipline and more in line with their own particular institution and a national perspective. These criteria are even set in terms of values, such as those in the UK developed by the ILTHE, and these suggest a restriction of individual autonomy over values (see Figure 6.2). The pressure on the academic to conform is increasing and the time available in which to make decisions about the values to adopt is decreasing. The old 'job for life' adage has long since disappeared from an academic's vocabulary.

The background context within which the different elements interact and influence the development and reinterpretation of an academic's values, and therefore ultimately his or her understanding of the scholarship of teaching, may have a profound influence. A

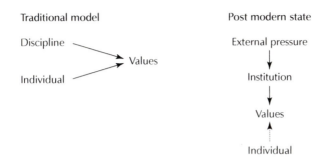

*Figure 6.2* Individual autonomy and values

cursory investigation suggests that interference and influence are more likely to occur in certain regions of the world (for example the UK and Australia) than others (such as the US). The result has been that although the concept of the scholarship of teaching has been embraced by academics in the US, the UK and Australia this has been for different reasons, with different expectations and with different views of the meaning that this conveys.

## Embracing the scholarship of teaching: an international perspective

The emergence of the concept of the scholarship of teaching in the United States has rapidly filtered across higher education and been readily embraced by many in the community, particularly within Australia and the UK. According to Gosling (2001: 78) this is indicative of a 'growing commitment to the importance of teaching and learning' and is a response to Elton's 1993 warning that teaching enhancement in universities was generally 'an activity conducted in private between two not always consenting adults' (p. 134). However, Lueddeke (2003: 213) reflects that 'While the rhetoric about teaching and learning is certainly in the right direction . . . one wonders whether much has really changed.' Resistance to change has been demonstrated by various stakeholders involved, the most obvious of these in the UK and Australia being government.

The consequences of the different stakeholders' involvement can be identified in the interpretation and understanding of the scholarship of teaching in the US and elsewhere. The differences are based upon both the context within which the debates are held and also how long these debates have been engaging their local academic communities. Some have argued that the context in the US is very much centred on what teachers do, whilst in Australia and Europe the focus has been upon students' learning. As stated in Chapter 2, the difference is often linked back to the influence of the German universities of the mid-nineteenth century, where the emphasis was on the discipline and not on the education of the individual. The US system reflects the German ethos by relating the scholarship of teaching to the individual teacher and the 'product' of the discipline they are engaged with, whereas the UK and Australian systems relate the scholarship of teaching more to the wider community, or institution, and concentrate very much on the 'process' of teaching as it relates to learning. Certainly the focus of much European and Australian writing is the complex relationship between teaching and learning (Ramsden 1992, Nicholls 2002). Central to Trigwell's (2001) model of university teaching is student learning. He suggests that there are a variety of issues that need to be included when considering teaching; these include the teachers' strategies, planning, thinking and the context. He concludes, 'good teaching is the effective application of a combination of a scholarly approach to teaching, and teaching plans and strategies that are derived from a student-focused conception of teaching' (p. 72). The logical next step is that the debate over the scholarship of teaching in the UK will turn into one based around the scholarship of learning.

Raising the debate has been important, as it has stimulated some significant discussions within higher education as to what the scholarship of teaching actually means. As Kreber (2002c) points out, the 1990s saw the implementation of initiatives to improve the quality of teaching and learning. In the US there has been a rapid growth in programmes relating to scholarship, many under the auspices of the Carnegie Foundation for the Advancement of Teaching. In 1998 the Carnegie Foundation in collaboration with the Pew Charitable Trusts launched the Carnegie Academy for the Scholarship of Teaching and Learning (CASTL). The CASTL strategy was aimed at advancing the scholarship of teaching and learning and bringing recognition and reward to teaching. The Pew Scholars National Fellowship Program created a community of more than one hundred fellows, whose role was to advance the profession of teaching and thereby enhance learning. Appointed for a year, these scholars are drawn from various disciplines and aim to provide clearer understanding of the scholarship of teaching. According to Glanville and Houde (2004), Shulman's efforts to develop peer collaboration further contributed to interest in the scholarship of teaching. The AAHE subsequently launched a national initiative to develop strategies via which academics could serve as peers to one another in teaching, just as many were already doing in research. This approach is now being established more widely in the university sector in the UK, although pressure for it came from external sources, namely government.

There have been some parallels in Australia and the UK. Andresen (2000: 24), reflecting on the situation in Australia, suggests that an increasing number of institutions are 'embracing the Boyerian stance and attempting to implement it in their policies'. In the UK programmes aimed at enhancing learning and teaching have been developed; the Institute for Learning and Teaching in Higher Education (ILTHE, which has now become part of the Higher Education Academy) accredited 164 programmes at 114 higher-education institutions (ILTHE 2003). As these programmes multiply, a growing number of bodies have become involved in the scholarship of teaching. A review by the Higher Education Funding Council for England (HEFCE 2003) found that these included: individual HE institutions, the ILTHE, Learning and Teaching Support Network and the Higher Education Staff Development Agency (HESDA). The interpretation of the scholarship of teaching appears to be being significantly influenced by institutions and agencies.

Perhaps inevitably, the different contexts for higher education generate different interpretations and create difficulty in establishing a universally accepted notion of the scholarship of teaching. Kreber and Cranton (2000) note what they believe is a major difference between the US and elsewhere. In the US the scholarship of teaching is viewed as an activity that takes place at the university but can also be related to an individual and the development of his or her career. As such the scholarship of teaching can be seen as a flexible, individualistic concept. They go on to suggest that the definition and understanding of this is more limited in the UK and Australia, where the focus has been restricted to the institution and the creation of an environment that supports teaching and learning. Such an interpretation is certainly supported by the evidence from Menand and Nixon, who, as outlined earlier, have suggested that in the UK the focus on individuality has been at the level of institutions rather than individual staff and students. Another difference that Kreber and Cranton (2000) note is that within the UK the debate is often located within the teaching and research continuum. In the US they suggest that there is an added element of 'service', meaning that an element of the academic's work is for the college, serving on committees, doing administration and providing external contributions within the local community.

According to McWilliam (2004), universities in the UK and Australia exhibit much more overt regulatory pressure from government than those in continental Europe or the United States. McWilliam argues that this is the result of a shift in the position of government in the UK and Australia from 'being patrons of universities to being buyers of higher education services and products' (p. 155). The shift has been created as a result of an examination by the universities of how to self-manage around the notion of 'risk'. Both the Higher Education Management Review Committee (see Hoare et al. 1995) in Australia and the Dearing Report (1997) in the UK highlighted the failure of the universities to develop an appropriate culture of self-regulation to ensure high performance.

Following the Dearing Report (1997) in the UK, Badley (2001) argues that it has become possible for enquiry to be held into teaching and learning within the disciplines and not merely by a small group of people possibly outside the front line of teaching. The danger is that whilst the higher-education community is reaching out to embrace the scholarship of teaching to enhance the status of a major aspect of the academic's role, the institutions and external agencies (such as government) hijack the increased interest and manipulate the meaning for their own ends. For example, in the UK, although there were probably traces of it prior to Callaghan's 1976 Ruskin Speech, it has since become evident that those within the teaching 'profession' should conform to government expectations (Shain and Gleeson 1999). The movement towards increased scrutiny into the work of academics in higher education has been fronted by calls for more openness and transparency about how public funds are spent. The result: an increasing preoccupation with indicators of performance and a desire to develop national professional standards. Intensified discourses of managerialism have developed an almost pathological requirement for standards and competencies in the UK, which has taken over the debate into what actually constitutes good teaching. It has been led not by values relating to the scholarship of teaching but by criteria or standards set by agencies (such as the ILTHE and the DfES) that distort the real meaning of scholarship by distilling it down to a series of bullet points that negate and fail to recognize the complexity of the relationships involved. These criteria or standards are given legitimacy by being couched in terms of professionalism. Even a cursory examination of recent government policy in the UK provides evidence. For example, *The Future of Higher Education* states:

> All providers should set down their expectations of teachers with reference to national professional standards; should ensure that staff are trained to teach and continue to develop professionally; should have effective quality assurance systems and robust degree standards; and should value teaching and reward good teachers.
>
> (DfES 2003: 4.14)

The UK has not been the only country to embrace a standards-driven agenda of enhancement in teaching and learning. Just as Badley recognized shifts in the UK, in Australia the development of the Australian Universities Teaching Committee in 2000 saw the beginning of reviews into teaching and learning within the disciplines. However, as Lynch et al. (2002) state, the reviews were evidence of an environment where interest was growing into what teaching was about and an attempt to evaluate this 'for the purpose of accountability'. Such a movement towards quality assurance within universities in Australia has led to further interest in the quality of teaching, rather than a philosophical interest in the scholarship of teaching per se.

A quick parallel can be drawn in the UK with the Research Assessment Exercise (RAE). According to Sullivan (2003) the RAE can be seen as a technicist task that constrains the work of the scholar. The purpose is to promote research by rewarding researchers in order for the research to carry on and develop – a self-perpetuation. The RAE is a method that enables a distribution of public funds based around criteria. The focus is on the end result. There is no assessment of personal qualities, the individual is depersonalized and the real significance of the research is neglected. Scholarship as defined earlier in this book as relating to discovery and innovation has little place here and yet it is the 'research' that is the recognized route for defining our understanding of the concept of scholarship.

Another interesting point is raised by McWilliam (2004), who points out that the increased number and diversity of the student population engaging in university study worldwide has created a challenge that traditional academic culture cannot meet. The reaction has not been to gain greater understanding of the concept of learning but rather to introduce audit regimes based around measurement and accountability to the extent that 'the craft knowledge of academics is being reshaped by administrative interventions that work to achieve fair and efficient institutional practice' (p. 156). The traditional role of academic scholarship is being displaced and an added dimension, an administrative professional expertise, is being integrated into the role.

## Strength in numbers: the need for consensus

According to Kreber and Cranton (2000) there are at least three perspectives on the meaning of the scholarship of teaching. The first suggests that it can be viewed in the same way as the traditional research model and that it is about discovery, innovation and the sharing of knowledge with peers and public. Such an interpretation does not require academics to be effective teachers themselves but merely to recognize and relay what it is to be an effective teacher to others. The interpretation fails to broaden the definition of scholarship as all it suggests is that the scholarship of teaching is research into teaching and as research is already recognized as part of the definition nothing is added. A second view provides the opposite interpretation by suggesting that the scholarship of teaching is recognized in practice by those engaging with the teacher. Within this definition there is no requirement for academics to regard teaching as a learning process for themselves, and one that they need to research. The only evidence of outstanding practice may be student evaluations or the occasional peer review and these are unlikely to be accepted as providing full and reliable evidence of the demands of scholarly work. A third interpretation combines the first two and argues that the scholarship of teaching requires the application of theory and research to an individual's own practice. Such a model is an examination of the process rather than the product of teaching and rests on being able to demonstrate scholarship that develops from an individual and that can be measured against the qualities and standards expected of scholarly work.

These are serious areas for concern. To be accepted as a relevant concept, the scholarship of teaching needs to be identified and subject to a common understanding. A danger of trying to pull disparate meanings together is that the conceptualization becomes reduced to 'meaningless jargon' that will lead to further rejection by many already disinclined to take note of educational literature. The notion of the scholarship of teaching, if it continues to be presented without a clear definition, will doubtless be judged as adding further to the myths surrounding education and merely be viewed as another 'heading' under which is addressed little of value or relevance. Unfortunately, as Healey (2000: 176) points out, the 'idea of scholarship in teaching is an attractive one to those who are keen to see improvement in the status of teaching in higher education institutions'. Although Elton and Partington (CVCP 1993: 9) note that currently 'scholarship is associated purely with research, when in fact it is just as relevant to teaching', Kreber (2002c) suggests that for teaching to be afforded the same status within higher education as research, the notion of the scholarship of teaching needs to be made real. If this is achieved and the concept gains acceptance as something that can be recognized and identified, those who can demonstrate it may gain the same rewards as those currently associated only with research.

Whatever the differences of focus and context between the US and other higher-education communities, the scholarship of teaching may appear to have helped fend off the challenges presented by those outside the profession. In other words the scholarship of teaching has provided the higher-education community with a potential professional value to relate to. There is a clear indication that the work of Boyer and his colleagues has created a shift in the US and to some degree in the UK and Australia. The notion of the scholarship of teaching has gained momentum. The American Association for Higher Education has taken the work of Boyer forward and expended a great deal of energy looking at roles and rewards for academics. The concept is at the forefront of many discussions on faculty development. This has led to increased calls from academics and academic developers in Australia and the UK for a similar approach to be introduced.

For those involved with the Carnegie Foundation who have spent a great deal of time examining the issues, the evidence would suggest that, whilst many may be excellent teachers, they will not have treated their teaching and learning environments as areas where enquiring into issues can and should be undertaken. To do this will require a real shift in culture and understanding. Although experts in their own particular field, many academics are uncertain how to use this knowledge to explore their practice within the area of teaching and learning. They understand what it is to know their subject, they know what it is to research and innovate within their discipline, but they cannot or do not currently translate this to their teaching. If the higher-education community is going to make the scholarship of teaching relevant to the values of the academic then it needs to be able to define what it means in order for it to be recognizable and useful to the academic community worldwide. If this is not done, the fragmentation of higher education and the fault lines that have appeared (Rowland 2002) will develop further. This will lead to the values that identify the role of an academic being constructed by an institutional context rather than by individuals and being based upon a notion of professionalism defined by external bodies. The academic will be left to pick up the pieces. As Nixon (2001: 175) ominously suggests:

> Long after the Institute for Learning and Teaching in Higher Education has specified its final standard of performance and calibrated its last outcome measure, academic workers will have to continue the struggle to be 'good' at their job: purposeful, morally alert, open to the unpredictability of learning.

The scholarship of teaching offers a way out, but it offers more than one route. It is up to members of the academic community to define which route applies to them.

*Part 3*

# Challenging the future

*Chapter 7*

# Scholarship: the challenge of the future

> Just because we cannot see clearly the end of the road, that is no reason for not setting out on the journey. On the contrary great change dominates the world and unless we move with change we will become its victims.
>
> (J.F. Kennedy)

The notion of the scholarship of teaching has been prevalent for the last decade, yet as more is published, more confusion grows as to the meaning of the concept and its relevance to the higher-education community. The scholarship of teaching represents a view of how teaching may be conceptualized into a more scholarly activity in higher education. Throughout the book Boyer's (1990) contribution to the scholarship debates within higher education has been referred to and discussed. This chapter re-examines such arguments, taking account of the ever-increasing complexity of higher education and the role that academics may have within that complexity. Particular attention is given to the role of learning within scholarship and higher education, not only for individual academics, but for the institutions in which they work and the more global structure in which they perform their duties.

The practice of research, scholarship and teaching in higher education and the role of learning for the academic within higher education are equally dependent on the whole educational context. Increased legislation and compliance in higher education in relation to the enhancement of teaching and learning require academics constantly to review how research, scholarship and teaching affect the role of learning for them in pursuit of their academic roles and responsibilities. This necessitates consideration of the role of the scholarship of teaching within an academic community that is constantly being asked to concentrate on research or teaching. Increasingly the academic is torn between scholarship, research and teaching, a situation not helped by the possibility of further polarizations whereby institutions will be able to gain university status for teaching only.

Boyer (1990) was one of the first to draw attention to the narrow conception of scholarship held by the profession.

> Scholarship is not an esoteric appendage; it is at the heart of what the profession is all about. All faculty, throughout their careers, should themselves remain students. As scholars they must continue to learn and be seriously and continuously engaged in the expanding intellectual world. This is essential to the vitality and vigour of the undergraduate college.
>
> (p. 56)

Given Boyer's emphasis on learning and the need to continue to learn, learning should form the key basis for discussions of the notion of scholarship. I suggest that academics should be focusing attention on understanding the meaning of the term 'scholarship' and on how this understanding can effectively contribute to a deeper recognition of academic activity. The research relating to the scholarship of teaching and the various forms of scholarship as identified by Boyer is plentiful and diverse in its interpretations. But what is the impact of dissecting scholarship into various definitions, meanings or forms? What consequences might this process of deconstruction have for academics trying to engage with scholarship in different institutions, which in themselves are trying to understand their nature and status as well as trying to adhere to external policies? A classic example of this is the dichotomy of research-led institutions versus teaching-led institutions, where academic roles are very often perceived differently, with differing priorities and expectations.

## The research-led university v. the teaching-led university

Research and research activity as measured by the Research Assessment Exercise (RAE) often direct actions and intent within a research-based institution. Teaching and teaching-based activities are often considered with equal intensity but not necessarily with equal importance. Hence, asking the question 'Why should academics in this environment be motivated to engage with the scholarship of teaching?' is highly relevant. Equally important is the reverse of this scenario. Within a teaching-based institution, teaching and teaching-based activities as measured by student retention dominate actions and intent. Research and research-based activities are often considered with equal intensity but not necessarily with equal importance. Hence, asking the question 'Why should academics in a teaching-intensive environment be interested in engaging in research relating to the scholarship of teaching?' is also highly relevant.

Why it is that scholarship is tied so closely to research rather than learning is an interesting issue. Scholars in the past, such as Nelson (1981), called for the renewal of the teacher-scholar. Nelson describes the ideal teacher-scholar in the following way:

> Ideally the college professor would be a widely respected scholar excited about learning and capable of communicating this excitement to others, a teacher deeply concerned with welfare of students and eager to have them learn and grow, one who teaches imaginatively both by books and by personal example, a demanding, very compassionate person who respects the moral worth of students and their potential growth.
>
> (p. 7)

As has been shown in previous chapters, present-day conceptions of scholarship are much too narrow. Increasingly the literature is arguing that there is a need to reconceptualize the meaning of scholarship within higher education (Kreber 2002a, Trigwell et al. 2000, Nicholls 2001). Rice (1992) suggests that during the expansion period in American higher education – what Jencks and Riesman (1968) called the 'academic revolution' – scholarship was equated with research and the cutting edge of a discipline. Further, it took on significance only when it was publishable in a refereed journal: one narrow facet of the scholarly enterprise, one way of knowing (p. 115).

In today's global society, with an ever-increasing demand and desire for knowledge, academics need to perceive scholarship in a wider context, one that allows for diversity of thought and accepts the expanding and changing demands of higher education. A view of scholarship that embraces the day-to-day working lives of the new generation of academics, one that very much includes learning and teaching.

Scholarship has increasingly returned to our vocabulary in higher education, particularly within the context of teaching. But why, when in some universities teaching is considered a derivative activity? The ideal teacher-scholar as described by Nelson is not the norm. At this juncture it is relevant to consider how the professionalization of the scholar has influenced the concept of scholarship being associated with research rather than teaching. Parsons (1968), in an essay on the professions, described the 'educational revolution that was occurring post world war two'. Fundamental to this revolution was the process of professionalization. Central to his argument was that a professionally orientated society needs the modern university, and 'the professional *par excellence* is the academic'. He defines this academic thus:

> The typical professor now resembles the scientist more than the gentleman-scholar of earlier times. As a result of the process of professionalisation, achievement criteria are now given the highest priority, reputations are established in national and international forums rather than locally defined, and the centre of gravity has shifted to the graduate faculties and their newly professionalised large-scale research function.
>
> (Parsons 1968: 36)

Parsons's description is very appropriate to what is happening globally. This notion of research excellence is disseminated in Britain through the Research Assessment Exercise (RAE). What is interesting about Parsons's statement is that it does not describe the typical professor. Rice (1992) suggests that what Parsons articulates is 'the dominant fiction by which academics measure themselves and their colleagues'. Rice goes on to argue that the image of the academic professor shapes the conceptions of a faculty and institutional policies to the extent that it determines promotion, tenure and sabbaticals. This perception of the academic remains and is at present dominant in higher education.

Finally, Rice articulates seven criteria that dominate the professional image of the academic:

1. Research is the central professional endeavour and the focus of academic life.
2. Quality in the profession is maintained by peer review and professional autonomy.
3. Knowledge is pursued for its own sake.
4. The pursuit of knowledge is best organised according to discipline (i.e. according to discipline-based departments).
5. Reputations are established through national and international professional associations.
6. The distinctive task of the academic professional is the pursuit of cognitive truth.

7. Professional rewards and mobility accrue to those who persistently accentuate their specialisation.

(p. 119)

These criteria are now well established and recognizable as elements of the academic's life.

Boyer's analysis of scholarship identifies four key roles: the scholarship of teaching, discovery, application and integration. Boyer considered teaching not simply as a matter of dissemination (transmission of knowledge) but as a form of scholarship. By this he meant transforming and extending knowledge through the process of classroom debate and a continual examination and challenge of both content and pedagogy.

Boyer's own beliefs regarding scholarship are worthy of repetition:

> We acknowledge that these four – the scholarship of discovery, of integration, of application and of teaching – divide intellectual functions that are tied inseparably to each other. Still there is value, we believe, in analysing the various kinds of academic work, while also acknowledging that they dynamically interact, formatting an independent whole.
>
> (Boyer 1990: 25)

Boyer's assertion allows us to look at scholarship in a broader context, thus enabling scholarship to be viewed as an interrelated whole with distinctive components and different approaches to knowing. The time has come to rethink what Boyer intimated by knowing and learning and propose that higher education should aspire to understand what learning is and how it affects roles and responsibilities within higher education.

The essence of higher education is, or should be, learning, from the senior research professor to the first-year undergraduate. All are expected to engage in the process of understanding, creating and applying knowledge. All should be involved in scholarship and the products of scholarship. Yet, as has been demonstrated throughout this book, the meaning of scholarship has not only changed over the centuries, but in some circumstances it has been usurped and even adjusted to mean something completely different. As Wittgenstein stated in his early writings (1953), 'Every word has a meaning. This meaning is correlated with the word.' It is the application of the word that provides the meaning: the context that is given or associated with it. The previous chapters have argued that with increased written discussion and interpretation of the word 'scholarship', particularly with respect to the term 'the scholarship of teaching', context, meaning and application have become the cornerstones of engagement and implementation. The activities that are deemed to constitute the scholarship of teaching vary so significantly that it reminds us of Locke's view that knowledge and understanding are often held back by words that have no fixed significance in their meaning. As a result the terms, in this case 'scholarship' and particularly 'the scholarship of teaching', have become beset with controversy and debate because of an unacknowledged ambiguity in how they are applied.

The key element in meaning is the understanding of the word by those engaging with it. I would like to suggest that there are four possible aspects that might help to contextualize scholarship and the variety of meanings it appears to be generating in current higher-education discourse, particularly with respect to teaching and the enhancement agenda within England. The four areas are:

1. understanding the role of scholarship
2. knowing and learning: an academic perspective
3. complexity, risk and the learning academic
4. understanding change: the role of scholarship.

## Understanding the role of scholarship

At the heart of being a professor is scholarship, i.e. the need to learn and know. For university academics, daily or very regular contact with the teaching, learning and research situation has always contributed to the development of discipline, scholarship and pedagogic knowledge. This being the case it is possible to suggest that academics have been involved in learning and the development of understanding and scholarship by the very nature of their positions and jobs. Learning is part of studying a specific discipline or subject and as such can be perceived as a privilege for those involved in higher education. Yet, in an academic community we still need to ask questions relating to the role of learning within the academy. A consequence of a variety of government initiatives, particularly within the UK, such as the Dearing Report (1997), the White Paper (2003) and the Higher Education Bill 2004, has been the need for the higher-education community to understand and debate the issues related to 'learning from learning' and how this may equate to scholarship. It is suggested that learning from learning is a key facet of development (Becher 1996, Jarvis 2002). In this context learning from learning is seen as having as its central concern the promotion and support of learning, not only of students, but also of academics themselves in their own personal research and teaching.

Research has shown that the ways in which teachers think about teaching substantially influences the approaches to learning adopted by students (Prosser and Trigwell 1997, Trigwell et al. 2000, Nicholls 2001, Kreber 2002a, 2002b). Research has also shown that academics' view of the nature of knowledge and the relationship of that knowledge to their teaching influences the extent to which they are prepared to innovate and learn from their teaching (Brew and Wright 1999, Nicholls and Jarvis 2002, Birgerstam 2002, Prosser et al. 2003). If learning is taken as a process of construction (Entwistle 1997, Biggs 1996, Prosser and Trigwell 1997), and of being involved with the creation of knowledge rather than simply absorbing it, then an alternative perspective can be given to academics learning from their research and teaching.

The concept of learning can be viewed as developing a personal understanding of the phenomena of research, scholarship and teaching, and of the links between them. The implication of this is that all three areas need to take account of how individuals develop their understanding of each phenomenon, as well as the conceptions that are being developed. Figure 7.1 shows how scholarship encompasses

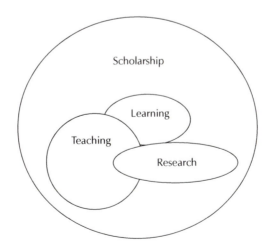

*Figure 7.1* Scholarship, learning, teaching and research

each element of learning. Key in this argument is that the academic has to understand that the relationship between learning, research, scholarship and teaching is dynamic and context driven. What is important here is that if such a process does not occur the individual is not engaged in learning and developing his or her own understanding of the concepts. This would suggest that if academics are to be learners, and learning is to be given value, learning opportunities that provide access and progression have to be actively and reflexively engaged in. Edwards (1997) suggests that focusing on the learner and learning requires a shift to reflexive learning, knowing and thinking which requires the academic to learn and understand the learning that has taken place.

## Knowing and learning: an academic perspective

> Learning flourishes when we take what we think we know and offer it as community property among fellow learners so that it can be tested, examined, challenged and improved before we internalise it.
>
> (Shulman 1999)

In his key address to the American Association of Higher Education (AAHE), Shulman raised the question of what we mean by 'taking learning seriously' within the higher-education community. Learning is a dual process in which the intended beliefs and understandings must be made explicit before anything new might be taken in and internalized. Effective learning is characterized by both the learner's awareness of his or her learning activity and the learner's ability to take action based on this reflection.

Learning with understanding is a 'sense-making' activity. Understanding develops as people use what they already know (i.e. prior knowledge) to construct meaning out of new information. Learning with understanding requires individuals to determine relationships and connections among new ideas and facts and prior knowledge. The process allows individuals to make sense of new information as their knowledge about a topic not only increases quantitatively, but changes qualitatively by becoming more differentiated and elaborate. The result is a representation or mental model that structures the conceptual knowledge. Dewey (1993) first described the process of learning with understanding as one in which the individual develops a well-differentiated, elaborate mental representation of the topic.

To grasp the meaning of a thing, an event or situation is to see it in its relations to other things; to note how it operates or functions, what consequences follow from it; what causes it can be put to. In contrast, what we call the brute thing, the thing without meaning, to us is something whose relations are not grasped.

(Dewey 1993)

Learning with understanding is a sense-making and knowledge-building process; as understanding develops, the learner's mental models of the subject matter become more highly differentiated. In academic settings, learning with understanding is sometimes effortless and straightforward. But often learning is slow and difficult, frequently more difficult than we accept, acknowledge or anticipate. Learning for understanding requires the learner to appreciate that they are in the process of learning by engaging with new knowledge; learning from the act of being engaged in the learning process is very important to development.

Accepting learning from learning requires academics to acknowledge that the different ways of learning and knowing exist and influence outcomes and have a significant role to play in understanding issues relating to scholarship, research and teaching. It is essential that the structure of knowledge and alternative approaches to learning are given a context and a constructive framework in which to operate. The literature on learning is vast, and a review of it suggests that the various dimensions of learning can be polarized into two categories: concrete-abstract and reflective-active. Such a polarization is a useful way of considering the type of learning that may contribute to academic learning and the role scholarship, research and teaching have in that learning.

Examining the first category of dimension, that of concrete-abstract, allows us to consider how knowledge is perceived. This is a key element in the discussion of learning within an academic domain. Within this context one aspect of an academic's world relates by definition to his or her discipline/knowledge base. Knowledge can be seen to have one pole which is dominated by the abstract-analytical approach, usually associated with academic research, where the learning focuses on objectivity and demands high levels of specialization from the individual, who takes pride in claiming that such knowledge is 'value free'. At the other end of this continuum knowledge is based on the concrete experience that is learned from contexts, relationships and valuing communities.

In order to conceptualize academic learning in this way it is necessary to consider the elements that may affect the role of the individual within the learning context. Three areas need to be considered, derived from Lortie (1975): the organizational, associational and professional elements of the academic's learning and understanding. The first aspect, organizational, relates to the role of the academic within the structural and policy-making framework of the state; the second considers the academic's response to issues of pay and conditions of work; the third relates to the academic's attempts to promote his or her role, autonomy and image. Scholarship is about learning and modes of learning. The previous chapters have suggested that scholarship and learning in higher education are shaped and influenced by the disciplines and the cultural structures in which the disciplines operate, as well as being influenced by the traditions of learning within the disciplines. What is missing from this focus is individual learning and autonomy.

Research, scholarship and teaching are about learning and modes of learning. At present these are shaped by the social structures in which they are located and by the influence of historical traditions of learning. What is missing from this is an element that allows the individual academic to focus on professional self-understanding and aims, as well as on the actual developments in education, work, markets and career progression for the members of the profession, in this case members of the academic community.

Birgerstam (2002) suggests that there are two different ways of acquiring knowledge, and that knowledge is something very complex and elusive. Acquiring meaningful knowledge and the ability to take action that carries the stamp of reality requires academics and students alike to understand the role of learning. Whether this be intuitive or rational, such understanding is essential for academics who deal with knowledge that is complex, problematizing and strategic. Birgerstam further argues that in order to deal with human nature and learning, it is important to understand, not only that which is relatively stable and general, but also that which is changeable, deviant, ambiguous and often contradictory.

For many academics the development of knowledge can start from well-defined goals and conditions based on the questions and issues. Here learning becomes primarily a rational activity in order to learn scientifically proven facts, find answers and make generalizations. However, knowledge can also develop from complex goals, ambiguous situations and vague or ill-defined questions – what Birgerstam considers complex phenomena (2002: 433). Within these contexts, how can academics be enabled to learn and reflect on how they have conducted their learning from complex points of departure? Equally important is how higher-education institutions can create learning situations for academics, so that they have the opportunity to develop their capacity to reflect and learn within research, scholarship and teaching.

## Complexity, risk and the learning academic

The performance of a complex system such as higher education and of particular academic communities within this system depends on how all the parts work together, not how each part performs when taken separately. This whole-system perspective is difficult for higher-education institutions and the academic communities within them. Higher education, and particularly the individual within it, has traditionally coped by breaking things down into separate functions and processes. Complexity is often managed by focusing on only one small area at a time. Breaking down academic activities in this way can achieve learning efficiencies. However, the hope that all these finely tuned processes and functions will add up to more efficient and profitable enterprises is seldom realized (Bellah 1996). Appreciating and working with complex interdependencies is very challenging. Higher education appears to have powerful values that include individual achievement, scholarship, research, scientific specialization and at times linear thinking, which appear at odds with focusing on a complex system. Learning to work with complexity requires more than changing what we do; it requires new learning and a shift of mind.

A variety of research approaches and techniques have sought to clarify conceptions about learning and to focus on learning with understanding. Central to this research has been the shift in meaning of 'knowing' from being able to store information and repeat it to being able to make critical use of it. This changing conceptualization of knowing has also had significant influence upon knowledge development, acquisition and application, and has added to the complexities academics face when trying to engage with the development of knowledge and their own understanding and learning within that development. Ewell (1997) suggests that to understand such complexities individuals need to gain insight into what is known about how learning occurs and lasts.

Knowledge can be developed when the academic engages in the critical study of theories and assertions, and clashes of ideas and logical reasoning, thus arriving at convergent results, non-contradictory assumptions relating to certain phenomena. Alternatively, knowledge can be developed when academics problematize what is known, what is obvious, and set questions from these premises. Gadamer (1997) suggests that problematizing relates to understanding differences and contradictions, not as a means of identifying carelessness or weakness, but as a means of reflecting on the underlying complexities of the issue or phenomenon being studied.

An interesting question to pose here is 'Why don't academics easily and comfortably engage in problematizing their own learning? Why is it that knowledge development within research is more widely reflected upon?' These are areas for speculation, particularly if Larsson's (1997) view is considered. He argues that if those involved in knowledge development examined how sometimes the most obvious opposites can be brought to yield greater understanding of phenomena and experience, this would allow for greater engagement in learning. The most obvious opposites in higher-education discussions are research and teaching, scholarship and learning.

The idea of problematizing the concepts of research, teaching, scholarship and learning is exciting and challenging. It would allow each concept to be examined from different and new perspectives, and would encourage learning from knowledge development. Learning strategies might be identified that would show how the knowledge-development process operates and what methods and techniques are learnt by academics engaged in the developmental process. These could then be used to identify what Schön (1983, 1991) describes as 'what to do' elements or 'ability to act' elements within the knowledge-development process. The key issue here is that learning is being considered as a process engaged in by academics and that in order to understand themselves as learners, they have to engage with new challenges and problems more systematically. This applies equally to teaching, research and scholarship. Currently the model can be conceptualized as in Figure 7.2, but we are suggesting it should be conceptualized as in Figure 7.3.

The issue at stake here is how we engage academics in these types of engagement. By this I mean that learning, teaching, research and scholarship are all equally complex concepts that require under-standing and conceptualizing. Barnett (2003) expresses the issue of complexity well:

Complexity is a situation in which the relevant entities and forces that affect one exceed one's capacities to understand them. The university, for instance, cannot fully comprehend all the entities and forces that affect it. . . . [A] situation of complexity is a multiplication of relevant features such that they escape anything approaching a complete understanding.

(Barnett 2003: 24)

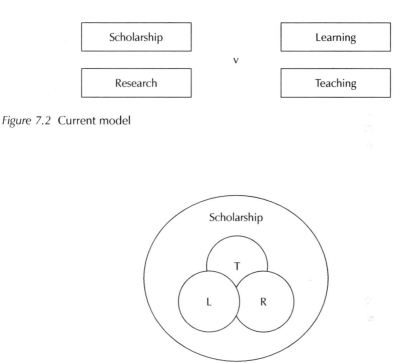

*Figure 7.2* Current model

*Figure 7.3* Suggested model

The tools of complex systems analysis provide the potential for identifying and understanding critical relationships within the academy that resist systemic change and afford new alternatives for considering scholarship and the role learning has within it. A common phenomenon in complex systems is that system behaviour is limited because some elements are decoupled from others; interactions that might otherwise be expected to occur are blocked or strongly buffeted. There are many examples of this in the present academy. In my research to date eight significant obstacles have been found with respect to scholarship, teaching, learning and research:

1. conflicting definitions of scholarship
2. implicit and explicit conceptions of what it means to be involved in conflicting scholarship within the academic community
3. conflicting conceptions of what it is to learn through scholarship, research and teaching
4. competition between colleagues for attention and prestige within a given field of study
5. lack of understanding of and empathy for institutional differences
6. incomplete implicit and explicit understandings of the expectations of scholarship
7. lack of a common communicative language within the academic community
8. lack of agreement within the community to collaborate in establishing a common understanding of scholarship.

Each of these obstructs the opportunity to unleash educational change by providing new channels for interaction. Overcoming each obstacle would be a significant step towards understanding change. As William Waller (1967) commented, 'Whatever contributes to understanding also contributes to reconstruction'. In even the most mature person, 'understanding is a mixture of insight and misconception, knowledge and ignorance, skills and awkwardness' (Wiggins 1998). However, within any changing situation there is risk. This cannot be ignored, particularly when the academic's role is changing more quickly than ever before.

## The complexity of risk within academic learning

I have argued elsewhere (Nicholls 2001) that the notion of risk is an important aspect of change, both of behaviour and learning situations. It is particularly relevant to the discussion here of the role academics must take in order to understand their own learning. D'Andrea and Quaranta (1999) suggest that risk factors do not possess, in and of themselves, the power to prevent the development of regimes; on the contrary, one might argue that risk factors generate reactions in individuals and encourage their consolidation into groups specifically aimed at controlling risk. The basis of this argument is that risk factors have three important distinctions: risk, danger and risk regime. The basic idea is that human societies and groupings always put up with harmful phenomena, constantly trying to keep them under control or to limit the danger they might cause.

To start with, since the nature of the outcome is often unknown, harmful phenomena tend to appear as dangers, and as such they are impossible to keep under control. However, once the danger is identified and becomes known, society or groupings tend to activate new regimes bent on exercising control and limiting the damage. New regulations are issued and initiatives promoted to inform people on how to face the danger, investments are made, actions are planned, and so on. In this way, a danger is gradually turned into a risk, i.e. an event or process potentially harmful but totally or partially kept under control. If one wanted to be cynical, this explanation of risk could be used to describe the enhancement agenda and the ever-increasing confusion in relation to scholarship. The harmful phenomena could be identified as the nexus between teaching and research, with the various groupings trying to keep the nexus under control by offering a variety of conceptualizations of how to limit the danger from increasing or decreasing the nexus. In fact, however, since this particular nexus was identified and publicized a variety of activities have been generated by new regimes, whether these are government initiatives or the educational development movement. There has been a direct set of actions aimed at exercising control and limiting the damage caused by the nexus. New initiatives have been introduced, such as the enhancement agenda in England and the faculty development movement in the US. These initiatives have respectively informed the academic community on how to face the nexus, invest in trying to change the nature of the nexus and create action plans in such a way as to turn the possible danger of the teaching-research nexus into a risk that can be potentially kept under control. The regimes that come into play are varied, depending on the risk factors that are taken into account. For example, government policies and investment, institutional cooperation, the academics within the institutions, and the nature of the institution can all be considered 'regimes of risk'. However, even more relevant are those regimes that people themselves produce by getting together and getting organized. These can be academic societies, associations and administrative alliances. These groupings arise from a need to reduce the risk as they perceive it.

D'Andrea et al. (1999) further argue that to understand the relationship between dangers, risks and risk regimes, a general theory of risk must be formulated and must take account of a second and particularly important dynamic, that of cumulative risk. This suggests that everyone, in this case the academic community, is in some way exposed to some risk factor; problems start when an increase in risk factors occurs within one area and the risks cascade. Individuals and groups exposed to the joint pressure of a multiplicity of risks find it increasingly difficult to react, and thus become weaker and weaker and increasingly less capable of producing regimes and managing them effectively. The consequence of these events is that the pressure within the community grows to a point of engendering confusion and possible poverty; here I mean 'poverty' with respect to the notion of what a university and an academic community involved in scholarship might represent or mean. This description can be applied to the dilemmas the higher-education community faces with respect to notions of scholarships, research and teaching and learning, particularly in England. Cumulative risk is real, and currently exists within the academic community. As Duderstadt (1999) suggests, 'scholarship may provide links in a sequence of political arguments, but scholarship run by political argument is fraught with too many risks. A group may benefit from scholarship, but scholarship with the explicit agenda of serving goals of a group is automatically suspect.'

The scholarship of teaching movement might well be considered to fall within Duderstadt's view. The scholarship of teaching was initiated as a mechanism to examine the theoretical underpinnings of teaching within a research discourse, but it gained momentum by trying to raise the status of teaching. Placing the focus of teaching within the context of scholarship and then the scholarship of teaching as a professional value has in many ways, wittingly or otherwise, exposed the whole of the academic community to the issues and risks surrounding scholarship, research and learning. Individuals and groups exposed to these new pressures find it increasingly difficult to react, and thus individual academics and groups such as educational developers and teaching enthusiasts feel they are in ever-weakening positions and unable to produce regimes for managing the situation more effectively. These pressures are increasingly manifesting themselves in how individuals assess the personal risk involved in engaging in activities such as the scholarship of teaching or investigating their own learning.

Fox (1999) puts forward a useful conceptualization of hazards and risk that allows us to consider the risk academics may have to take if they are to engage with their own learning strategies and mechanisms. Fox argues that 'risks (hazards) are socially constructed: created from the contingent judgements about the adverse or undesirable outcomes of choices made by human beings. These "hazards" are then invoked discursively to support estimations of risk, risky behaviour and of the people who take the risks' (p. 19). What does this mean for the academic wanting to understand his or her learning?

Consider the issue of an established academic wishing to understand why some concepts taught to his students are continuously misunderstood or misrepresented by them. In and of themselves, students' misunderstandings and misrepresentations do not constitute a threat to the established academic. They only become a risk under certain circumstances, principally if they cause the students to fail aspects of a programme or achieve a lower than expected degree classification. With increased scrutiny of student performance and academic performance this could be construed as a risky situation, as failure or low achievement can be appraised as an undesired or adverse outcome for both academic and student.

Transforming student behaviour and student learning is multifaceted and complex. Interrogating one's teaching as a means of critical enquiry and a strategy by which one can learn is a difficult approach for academics to accept, as Bradley (2002) suggests: 'like Barnett, I doubt that many teachers in higher education will take the harder option of seeing students as co-researchers and teaching as a form of critical enquiry. Most I imagine will continue to see teaching's role as the transmission of what is currently thought to be known' (Bradley 2002: 455). If Bradley's assertion is correct, critical enquiry into one's teaching as a form of learning becomes a significant risk to the academic. However, not accepting that change in delivery is required may also constitute a risk. What does risk analysis mean for academics who wish to engage in understanding how they teach and why they teach the way that they do, and to learn from the examination of these issues?

Analysis of risk revolves around the hazard that can or may come into existence through completing a task or set of actions. If the risk of not enquiring critically into one's teaching and learning is perceived as zero it is unlikely that academics will engage in any analysis of their teaching or of the mechanisms and strategies they use to learn. There lies the nub of the problem. How do we encourage academics to become learners in all aspects of their work, be able to identify how they learn, understand how they learn, reflect on that learning and use the newfound knowledge in helping their students to learn more effectively?

Appreciating degrees of risk at both personal and institutional levels requires academics and their host institutions to accept the complexities of the academic life, not just as researchers, but also as learners in their own right. It also requires higher education as a community to accept the complexities of those who work within the community. Learning to learn is not a new concept in education or psychology, yet there is very little recognition that learning from learning is a key aspect of scholarship. Maybe it is time to reconsider the work of academics within the learning institution that has to change.

## Understanding change: the role of scholarship

The difficulty in understanding change and coming to terms with its implications is well recounted in a story by Ringel (2000):

> As I think about change in our nation's universities and colleges, I am reminded of a wonderful story about a man and his wife who were shopping. The man picked up a shirt with a label on it that said 'shrink resistant'. He asked his wife what that meant. 'It means,' she said, 'that it will shrink but it doesn't want to.'
>
> (p. 1)

Ringel asserts that change and resistance to change constitute a dilemma that we face every day. Change is a non-avoidable part of our lives; it is quite simply a case of 'change or be changed' and the solution is not to try to suppress change, which cannot be done, but to manage it. But managing change also requires reference points and human involvement. Bennis (1973) suggests that 'change occurs in two primary ways, through trust and truth or dissent and conflict . . . The challenges to the organisation then are to create an environment in which trust and truth can flourish and thereby lead to a constructive process of change'.

Changing educational ideas and attempting to change educational perspectives is not easy at any time (Cuban 1990, Fullan 1991, 2002). It is particularly difficult when change involves a reconceptualization of roles, responsibilities and values within frameworks that have existed for a long time and are often seen as immovable. Scholarship, research and teaching fall very much within this bracket. Introducing new ideas and terms such as 'the scholarship of learning' becomes increasingly difficult in an environment that does not want, or is frightened to accept, new visions of learning and scholarship. As Fullan (2002) suggests, 'Good ideas with no ideas on how to implement them are wasted ideas'. Understanding change and its implications for the nature of scholarship within the academy requires academics to take stock of their position both as academics and as instruments of change within the academy itself. In today's world of higher education there is an array of powerful social, economic and technological forces driving change.

In Chapter 2 it was suggested that both the need to change and the anxiety caused by this need relate to the explosion in the information highway, reducing the individual scholar's ability to be familiar with all aspects of his or her discipline. Acceptance has been slow within the academy that the age of information is creating a knowledge-based society that depends heavily on the creation and application of new knowledge, and where the key strategic resource necessary for prosperity has become knowledge itself, that is, educated people and their ideas. Duderstadt (1999) argues that the more knowledge is used the more it multiplies and expands, and that knowledge is not available to all. It can be absorbed and applied only by the educated mind. Hence, as society becomes ever more knowledge-intensive, it becomes ever more dependent on those social institutions, such as the university, that create knowledge, educate people and provide those people with learning resources throughout their lives. Yet in an increasingly knowledge-driven society, more people seek education. The knowledge created within universities also addresses the needs of society, including health care and economic competitiveness. Through all this there is increased unease within the academy. Globally there has been an erosion of support for important university commitments such as academic freedom, with the result that academics are increasingly feeling stressed, fearing a decline in public support for research, sensing a loss of scholarly community with increasing disciplinary specialization, and being pulled out of the classroom and laboratory by the demands of research and gaining research funds. Could this explain the willingness of some members of the academic community to embrace the idea of the scholarship of teaching, which provides another defence against a loss of status for the profession and against challenges to its authority?

Universities are responding to these challenges, but most are doing so within the traditional definitions of their roles. As Duderstadt (1999) comments, 'most are evolving according to the time-honoured process of considered reflection and consensus that has long characterized the academy' (p. 3). But is this characterization sufficient for dealing with rapid change and ever-growing expectations for the academy to change? Some may say that change has always characterized the university, even as it has sought to preserve and propagate the intellectual achievements of civilization. However, equally it can be said that most changes in universities, although important, have been by and large reactive rather than strategic. Higher education still has not fully grasped the implications of a society for learning that is most likely to represent the future. Universities need to understand how to respond to the needs of a culture of learning if the future challenges of a knowledge-intensive society are to be met. Learning in itself, and learning within a higher education environment, are complex for student and scholar alike. Dixon (1994: 23) neatly summarizes the need for organizational learning when she states that 'the essence of organisational learning is the organisation's ability to use the amazing mental capacity of all its members to create the kind of processes that will improve its own learning capacity'. What context could be more appropriate than an academic community, whose mission it is to be involved in learning? As Senge (1990) suggests, the place where people continually expand their capacity to create the results they truly desire, where new expansive patterns of thinking are nurtured, where collective aspirations are set free, and where people are continually learning to learn together is the place that should drive a culture of learning and change.

Senge's sentiments suggest that learning is central to change and understanding the change that is required, as well as the nature of the engagement that has to take place in order for the change to happen. This type of learning is paradoxical, as Jarvis (1992) eloquently argues: 'learning is about becoming a person in society, about transforming experiences into knowledge, skills and attitudes so that individuals may develop; paradoxically, learning is also about adapting and becoming a conforming member of society' (p. 237). Here society can mean the higher-education community as well as society at large.

The challenge is to allow individuals to learn within a community that accepts learning to be the right of all involved in higher education.

*Chapter 8*

# Scholarship: a hostage to fortune

## Challenging scholarship

This book has attempted to provoke debate, rouse strong feeling and draw a response. To achieve this it has asked some important questions. We have challenged the notion of scholarship as it is currently understood, because the current understanding provides no foundation for answers to questions that are of fundamental importance to the future of higher education. Without these answers there is little optimism for the future of scholarship within the higher-education community. Fragmentation will increase and academics will barricade themselves on ever-shrinking islands of knowledge. But there is another way. Scholarship has been within the academy since its inception and there it should remain.

The book has outlined a series of debates and ideas concerning the future of scholarship within the higher-education community. These debates suggest how we may address issues related to teaching and learning through concepts such as the scholarship of teaching.

The previous chapters have identified problematic areas and issues, but some distinct benefits have also emerged, particularly concerning the continuum of learning and the role scholarship may play within that continuum. The definitions of scholarship seem on the surface to be less controversial, or are at least less contested; whereas the forms under which scholarship is organized and used as a tool for power and strategic positioning are more debatable. Any conversation about scholarship is bound to reach disagreement rather than consensus. However, as the discussion throughout this book has shown, two parameters can be identified within which the discourse of scholarship may shed light on its meaning and its representation.

The first has been defining scholarship, and the second is related to the question why academics and the academic community engage with scholarship. It is clear that academics and communities of scholars engage in scholarship for a variety of reasons, including the advancement of knowledge, participating in the scholarly conversations in their fields, to publish, to enhance teaching, to engage in continued learning and to obtain reward. These elements are particularly striking within the established disciplines in higher education. Chapter 5 concentrated on the issues of power base and knowledge development, arguing that it is in the interest of the disciplines and specializations within those disciplines to maintain their discrete boundaries of knowledge and associated mechanisms for teaching and learning. It was further suggested that the interest in maintaining boundaries was to continue disciplinary strongholds, attitudes and power bases. Although advantageous with respect to continuing frontline research, it is potentially not in the interest of the students' or academics' own learning to uphold rigid boundaries. Understanding and accepting alternative scholarly approaches is thought to be a useful challenge for any academic. This is particularly pertinent as recently there has been an apparent shift in paradigms, a shift that indicates a desire to explore and present a more coherent, contextual and holistic world-view, one that requires an exploration of the various forms of scholarship and interdisciplinary learning as a means of understanding how to rejoin a quest for knowledge. As Cummings (1989) argues:

> to create a unity of representations requires a carefully structured dialogue between the sectors of research and communication and between the production and consumption of knowledge, where in the past false dichotomies have marred practices. Increased internationalisation and quicker dissemination of knowledge facilitates a more integrative approach between scholars, universities, academic activities, research agencies and scholarly communities.

Yet, as we have demonstrated, this increase in knowledge and in the speed with which knowledge can be disseminated can cause further boundaries and fragmentation within the academic community.

# Scholarship as a means of challenging core values

We have chosen to discuss scholarship as a means of understanding universities' and their communities' relationships with the academics themselves, with universities' stakeholders, and with society at large, as these relationships bear upon the universities' definition of their purpose, the way they organize and understand their scholarly role and the impact they have on knowledge and learning. It is important to recognize and understand how exchanges between university scholarship and the surrounding society change with the changing values of higher education.

The core values of higher education are shifting; one could argue that over time these values have always been shifting and that each shift reflects a period of change. Currently what is interesting is the political force that is pushing and guiding such change within the higher-education sector in the UK, which is not quite the case universally. Chapter 4 demonstrates how identifying core values such as those described by the ILTHE, and particularly the core value of 'the scholarship of teaching', causes confusion within the higher-education community, not only through misinterpretation of the core values, but also through a lack of understanding of them and a resulting lack of engagement with them. More problematic still is that often the stated core values are assumed to be accepted throughout higher education and to be implicit in the behaviour of academics – an assumption which is currently misconceived. This is not to say that an agreed set of core values could never be established, but the higher-education community is currently so diverse in its approach, mission statements, focus and purpose that it is difficult to see how acceptable core values could be attained, particularly in a competitive higher-education system.

The core values are currently seen as part of an 'association' that comes from a framework of rules and procedures. As Hobbes argued in his writings, these rules and procedures are sanctioned by those exercising or attempting to exercise power and control. Hobbes argued that within this system individuals will continue to pursue self-interested goals. The key is for scholarship to be drawn away from this interpretation and for it to be seen as creating the possibility of morality within the academic community, as Rousseau would offer. Within this framework the core values associated with scholarship would allow the individual to visualize the interests outside him or herself, in the welfare of the academic community and all those involved in learning. A difficulty arises when we consider how people view their association with the 'academic community'. As has been suggested earlier in this book, the postmodern society has caused instability for those in the profession and the response has been to survive and to reduce the risks that can be recognized. To this end false communities are formed. As a result when academics are asked what community they belong to, their answers, even when couched in similar language, may mean very different things.

What have you got to lose? This is an important question to answer. Consider the experienced academic and the novice. Experienced scholars have their experience to lean upon, their values set over time and their opinions of scholarship as it relates to their disciplines and institutions. The novice has only uncertainty. Each individual is at some point upon this journey from novice to experienced scholar. Scholarship should be a unifying factor for each member of the academy and yet it is not. It gains widest acceptance when related to a particular field of research, and yet this limits the meaning of the concept. If scholarship is about innovation and universities are about imagination then scholarship should be explained by teaching and research. The art of discovery is found in both teaching and research and is understood through learning. It is through learning that scholarship may be explained. The debates surrounding the scholarship of teaching are misleading because, as argued in this book, they are not about scholarship. They are about professional shared values that are based on fixed criteria and not developmental aspects. The scholarship of teaching is a distraction from the underlying debate over the understanding of scholarship.

## Recent influences

The publication of the recent consultation document on professional standards for teaching and learning (HEFCE 2004) could be conceived as a turning point in higher education in the UK. It represents a step towards a much-needed holistic approach to a common set of understandings and expectations of teaching and learning within the academic community. It is a shame that the documentation is presented as a set of standards rather than core values, as standards often intimate a mechanistic approach to understanding performance, and that performance is then assessed against a series of competencies, reducing the process to one of compliance rather than development.

The current environment of consultation should be grasped by higher education and used to turn a possibly mechanistic approach to teaching, learning and the scholarly activities attached to such enterprises into a purposeful developmental and educative process of change within the community. There is a significant difference between compliance through mutual development and understanding, and compliance through imposition. The consultation is an opportunity for higher education to position scholarship at the heart of the academic's world, and it would be a shame to see this opportunity lost through a too-resigned acceptance of compliance. It could be argued that change will require not only political will but a paradigm and value-systems shift within higher education.

Scholarship is what academics are expected to be immersed in and yet the academic community appears unable to define what this is. As the academic community ponders how to respond, society, through government and public bodies, has stepped in and started to put a framework in place. The academic community needs to wake up and realize that through design or default such an approach will lead to a false interpretation of scholarship based on core values that are reliant on competency and compliance rather than development and defiance. Scholarship is currently a hostage to fortune, but it can be released and the possibilities of such freedom are worth the risks.

*Chapter 9*

# Final comments

To the casual observer it may appear that the meaning expressed by the word 'scholarship' has fluctuated and broadened through time. However, it is the understanding associated with the general term 'scholarship' that appears to have altered and the alteration may be a result of the context within which it is utilized. Two important points are raised here. The first is whether the meaning has changed. If it has, the second question that comes into focus is how much contextual issues have been responsible for the production of this altered understanding.

Has the meaning denoted by the term 'scholarship' changed? An initial point is to ask whose understanding it is that may have changed: those who undertake the scholarship or those on the receiving end of scholars' activity, the public. The academic community has always been associated with scholarship and this was relatively unchallenged through time until the twentieth century. The audience to which an understanding of the term is now applied has grown. Although the term 'scholarship' is still seen to apply broadly to those working in the academic community, understandings of the term are defined by those outside (the public) as well as inside this community. As we have seen earlier in this book, the professions are no longer free to act in isolation as they deem appropriate. The society within which these professionals operate now has a far greater impact upon the work they undertake. Whilst this may have many positive aspects to it, there is a danger that it has brought about the restriction of innovation. As innovation is a key aspect of the role of the scholar, the academic community could be expected to resist this change.

Greater involvement of the public has therefore altered our understanding of 'scholarship'. The audience is interested not only in listening to what the scholar has to say but in voicing its own interpretation. The understanding of both the scholar and the audience is clearly important. A central theme of this book has been that the academic community has to some extent lost its voice. The result has been a distortion of meaning, decreased certainty among those within the academic community about what scholarship actually means to them, and a reduced ability to reject definitions imposed by outside sources such as government. This book is not suggesting that the academic community should not engage in negotiations over meaning and that the public has no right to play a part; it does and it should. The danger is that without acknowledging the impact that the process is having, the understanding of general terms such as 'scholarship' becomes distorted by explanations that are not fully grounded in understanding.

To understand a term we need to know how it behaves in a wide range of circumstances. When we understand the term fully we can then use it to its full effect. The problem that has been identified in this book is that there is no understanding of scholarship and even less of the scholarship of teaching. As the professions are no longer able to put up the shutters to the outside world, the meaning of scholarship is defined by an increasingly diverse and complex group. It follows that gaining full understanding is likely to be extremely difficult. The remedy has been for those in administration to provide criteria and a structure by which all those involved can achieve common understanding. These criteria suggest that meaning can be achieved by a checklist.

Without a clear meaning, explaining the actions of a scholar is impossible. As Chart (2000: 5) argues, understanding the meaning of a term allows us to explain to others and as a result uncover 'human thought and the process of scholarship'. Chart identifies a difficulty when the focus is upon explanation rather than understanding. He argues that we can only explain something effectively when we understand it. The explanation then provides a clearer understanding. The chapters in this book have suggested that the understanding of scholarship has altered. Attempts have been made to explain what it is without fully understanding it.

The meaning of scholarship has changed over time and this book has offered an explanation of these changes. Attention has also been paid to how much impact context has had on the amount of change and how this has taken place. The postmodern society consists of 'super-complex' structures attempting to provide human beings with constants and the ability to feel 'safe' by means of prediction. Providing sufficient understanding to enable explanation of any term is immediately called into question in such a postmodern state. For instance, people may claim that they understand a person or an object such as an aeroplane and then claim not to understand the same thing (or some aspect of the same thing). Why should scholarship be any different?

A danger is that superficial understanding is provided that is only relevant in a certain context at a particular point in time. This causes confusion. To the casual glance all appears well but misunderstanding occurs and society moves further away from being able to explain and improve understanding. For example, scholarship was originally understood to relate to teaching. By the middle of the twentieth century this had been replaced by understanding scholarship as research. Towards the end of the century Boyer brought in the scholarship of teaching. At first glance the scholarship of teaching may appear to involve the same understanding of scholarship with a new application, but this book has shown that this is not the case. A new term has been born, which has complicated matters. It has not aided our explanation of scholarship or enabled greater understanding.

Scholarship has been defined by relating it to teaching and research. The above argument suggests that explaining scholarship by using teaching and research is a reasonable undertaking. However, these explanations can only be appropriate and real if the underpinning understanding of scholarship is accepted. This book has shown that it is not.

# Bibliography

Adams, D. (1998) Examining the fabric of academic life: an analysis of three decades of research on the perceptions of Australian academics about their roles, *Higher Education*, 36, pp. 421–435

Allen, K.E. (2002) The purpose of scholarship: redefining meaning for student affairs, *NASPA Journal*, 39, 2, pp. 147–157

Anderson, J.R. (1980) *Cognitive Psychology and its Implications* San Francisco: W.H. Freeman

Andresen, L.W. (2000) Teaching development in higher education as scholarly practice: a reply to Rowland et al. 'Turning academics into teachers?' *Teaching in Higher Education*, 5, 1, pp. 23–31

Andresen, L.W. (2000) A useable, trans-disciplinary conception of scholarship, *Higher Education and Development*, 19, pp. 137–153

Archer, M. (1984) *Social Origins of Educational Systems* London: Sage

Aristotle (1941) *Nichomachean Ethics* (trans. W.D. Ross). In R. McKeon (ed.) *Basic Works of Aristotle* New York: Random House

Aristotle (1996) *The Internet Encyclopaedia of Philosophy*, (online) http://www.utm.edu/research/iep/a/aristotle.htm

Astin, A. (1990) Faculty cultures, faculty values. In W.G. Tierney (ed.) *Assessing Academic Climates and Cultures* San Francisco: Jossey-Bass, pp. 61–74

Astin, A. & Baldwin, R. (1991) Faculty collaboration: enhancing the quality of scholarship and teaching, *ASHE-ERIC Higher Education Report No.7* Washington DC

Badley, G. (2001) Towards a pragmatic scholarship of academic development, *Quality Assurance in Education* 9, 3, pp. 162–170

Badley, G. (2003) Improving the scholarship of teaching and learning, *Innovations in Education and Teaching International*, 40, 3, pp. 303–309

Bamber, V. (2002) To what extent has the Dearing policy recommendation on training new lecturers met acceptance? Where Dearing went that Robbins didn't dare, *Teacher Development*, 6, 1, pp. 433–456

Barnet, B (1992) Teaching and research are inescapably incompatible, *Chronicle of Higher Education*, 38 (June 3, 1992): A40

Barnett, R. (ed.) (1994) *Academic Community: Discourse or Discord?* London: Kingsley

Barnett, R. (1994) *Recovering an Academic Community: Above But Not Beyond R* Buckingham: OU Press/SRHE

Barnett, R. (2000) *Realizing the University in an Age of Supercomplexity* Buckingham: OU Press/SRHE

Barnett, R. (2003) *Beyond All Reason: Living with Ideology in the University* Buckingham: OU Press/SRHE

Bauman, Z. (1992) *Intimations of Postmodernity* London: Routledge

Bauman, Z. (1999) *In Search of Politics* Cambridge: Polity Press

Baume, C. (1999) Professionalism in teaching. In Open University course H852, Course Design in Higher Education. Milton Keynes: OU Press

Baxter, M.M. & Terenzini, P.T. (2002) *Learning and Teaching in the 21st Century* ACPA. http://www.acpa.nche.edu/seniorscholars/trends/trends4.htm

Becher, T. (1987) The disciplinary shaping of the professorate. In B. Clark (ed.) *The Academic Profession: National, Disciplinary and Institutional Settings* Berkeley: University of California Press, pp. 271–303

Becher, T. (1989) *Academic Tribes and Territories* Buckingham: OU Press/SRHE

Becher, T. (1990) The counter-culture of specialisations, *European Journal of Education*, 75, pp. 333–346

Becher, T. (1994) Quality assurance and disciplinary differences, *Australian Universities Review*, 37, pp. 4–7

Becher, T. (1994) Interdisciplinarity and community. In R. Barnett (ed.), *Academic Community: Discourse or Discord?* Higher Education Policy Series 20. London: Jessica Kingsley, pp. 55–71

Becher, T. (1995) The internalities of higher education, *European Journal of Education*, 30, 4, pp. 395–406

Becher, T. (1996) The learning professions, *Studies in Higher Education*, 21, 1, pp. 43–57

Becher, T. (1997) The hunting of the gilt edged degree. In J. Brennan, P. De Vries & R. Williams (eds) *Standards and Quality in Higher Education* London: Jessica Kingsley, pp. 157–169

Becher, T. & Trowler, P. (2001) *Academic Tribes and Territories*, 2nd edn Buckingham: OU Press

Beck, U. (1992). *Risk Society* London: Sage

Bellah, R.N. (1996) Creating transforming communities. Unpub. paper presented at the annual conference of the association of Presbyterian Colleges, USA

Bennis, W. (1973) *The Learning Ivory Tower* San Francisco: Jossey-Bass

Benowitz, S. (1995) Wave of the future: interdisciplinarity collaborations, *The Scientist*, 9, 13 (Jan. 1995), pp. 1–5

Biggs, J. (1996) Enhancing teaching through constructive alignment, *Higher Education*, 32, pp. 347–364

Biglan, A. (1973a) The characteristics of subject matter in different scientific areas, *Journal of Applied Psychology*, 57, pp. 195–203

Biglan, A. (1973b) Relationships between subject matter characteristics and the structure and output of university departments, *Journal of Applied Psychology*, 57, pp. 204–213

Birch, W. (1988) *The Challenge to Higher Education* Milton Keynes: OU Press/SRHE

Birgerstam, P. (2002) Intuition – the way to meaningful knowledge, *Studies in Higher Education*, 27, 4, pp. 431–444

Blake, N., Smith, R. & Standish, P. (1998) *The Universities We Need: Higher Education after Dearing* London: Kogan Page

Bland, C. & Schmitz, C.C. (1990) A guide to the literature on faculty development. In J.H. Schuster & D. W. Wheller (eds) *Enhancing Faculty Careers: Strategies for Development and Renewal* San Francisco: Jossey-Bass

Boudon, R. (1986) *Theories of Social Change* Cambridge: Polity Press

Boulding, K.E. (1977) Peace research, *International Social Science Journal*, 29, pp. 601–614

Bourdieu, P. (1986) The forms of capital. In J. Richardson (ed.) *Handbook of Theory and Research for the Sociology of Education* New York: Greenwood Press

Bourdieu, P. (1988) *Homo Academicus* (trans. P. Collier) Cambridge: Polity Press

Bourdieu, P. (1989) For a socio-analysis of intellectuals: on homo academicus, *Berkeley Journal of Sociology*, 34, pp. 1–29

Bourdieu, P. (1993) *Sociology in Question* (trans. R. Nice) London: Sage.

Bourdieu, P. (1994) *Academic Discourses* Cambridge: Polity Press.

Bourdieu, P. (1998) *Practical Reason* Cambridge: Polity Press.

Bourdieu, P. & Wacquant, L. (1992) *An Invitation to Reflexive Sociology* Cambridge: Polity Press

Boyer, E. (1987) *College: The Undergraduate Experience in America* New York: Harper & Row

Boyer, E. (1990) *Scholarship Reconsidered* Washington, DC: Carnegie Foundation

Boys, M. (1999) Engaged pedagogy: dialogue and critical reflection, *Teaching Theology and Religion*, 2, 3, pp. 129–136

Bradley, G. (2002) A really useful link between teaching and research, *Teaching in Higher Education*, 7, 4, pp. 443–455

Braxton, J., Luckey, W. & Helland, P. (2002) *Institutionalising a Broader View of Scholarship through Boyer's Four Domains* San Francisco: Jossey-Bass

Breakwell, G. (1986) *Coping with Threatened Identities* London: Methuen

Brew, A. & Wright, A. (1999) Research and teaching: changing relationships in a changing context, *Studies in Higher Education*, 24, pp. 291–303

Buchanan, J.M. (1982) The domain of subjective economics: between predictive science and moral philosophy. In I.M. Kirzner (ed.) *Methods, Process and Austrian Economics* Lexington, MA: Lexington Books, pp. 7–20

Cameron, J.M. (1978) *On the Idea of a University* Toronto: St. Michael's College, University of Toronto Press

Carnegie Foundation. Approaching the scholarship of teaching and learning. Carnegie Foundation eLibrary. http://carnegie.foundation.org/elibrary/docs/htm

Chait, R.P. (1997a) Rethinking tenure: towards new templates for academic employment, *Harvard Magazine*, 99, 6, pp. 30–31

Chait, R.P. (1997b) Thawing the cold war over tenure, *Trusteeship*, 5, 3 (May/June 1997), pp. 11–15

Chart, D. (2000) *A Theory of Understanding* Aldershot: Ashgate

Clark, B. (1983) *The Higher Education System: Academic Organisations in Cross-National Perspectives* Berkeley: University of California Press

Clark, B. (1987) Conclusions. In B. Clark (ed.) *The Academic Profession: National, Disciplinary and International Settings* Berkeley: University of California Press, pp. 371–399

Cobbs, P. & Bowers, J. (1999) Cognitive and situated learning perspectives in theory and practice, *Educational Researcher*, 28, 2, pp. 4–15

Craft, A. (2000) *Continuing Professional Development* London: RoutledgeFalmer.

Cross, P. (1990) Teachers as scholars, *AAHE Bulletin*, 43, 4, pp. 3–5

Cross, P. & Steadman, M. (1996) *Classroom Research: Implementing the Scholarship of Teaching* San Francisco: Jossey-Bass

Cuban, L. (1990) Reforming again, again, again, and again, *Educational Researcher*, 19, pp. 3–13

Cummings, R.J. (1989) The interdisciplinary challenge, *National Forum*, 69, pp. 2–3

CVCP (1993) *Teaching Standards and Excellence in Higher Education* Sheffield: CVCP

Davidson, T. (1900) *Aristotle and the Ancient Education Ideal* New York: Charles Scribner's

Davis, J.R. (1995). *Interdisciplinarity Courses and Team Teaching: New Arrangements for Learning* Phoenix: Oryx Press

D'Andrea, L. & Quaranta, G. (1999) *Social Exclusion and Civic Society* vol. 1 Rome: CERFE

D'Andrea, L., Quaranta, G. & Quinte, G. (1999) Social Risk Analysis (SRA): theoretical foundations, application strategies and research perspective. In *Social Exclusion and Civic Society* vol. 1 Rome: CERFE

Dearing Report (1997) National Committee of Inquiry into Higher Education (NCIHE): *Higher Education for a Learning Society* London: HMSO

Delanty, G. (2001) *Challenging Knowledge: The University in the Knowledge Society* Buckingham: Open University Press

Dewey, J. (1993) *How We Think* Chicago: Regency

De Wulf, M. (1956) *An Introduction to Scholastic Philosophy* New York: Dover

DfES (2003) *The Future of Higher Education* Norwich: HMSO

Dill, D.D. (1991) The management of academic culture: notes on the management of meaning and social integration. In J.L. Bess (ed.) *Foundations of American Higher Education* Needham Heights, MA: Ginn Press, pp. 567–579

Diamond, R.M. (1993) The tough task of reforming the faculty rewards system, *Chronicles of Higher Education*, 40 (11 May 1994), pullout section

Dirks, A.L. (1998) *The New Definition of Scholarship: How Will It Change the Professoriate?* http://webhost.bridgew.edu/adirks/ald/papers/skolar.htm

Dixon, N. (1994) *The Organisational Learning Cycle* New York: McGraw-Hill

Donald, J.G. (2002) *Learning to Think: Disciplinary Perspectives* San Francisco: Jossey-Bass

Downie, R. (1990) Professions and professionalism, *Journal of Philosophy of Education*, 24, 2, pp. 147–59

Duderstadt, J.J. (1999) The future of higher education: new roles for the 21st century university, *Issues in Science and Technology on line* (winter 1999)

Durkheim, E. (1912/1965) *The Elementary Forms of Religious Life* New York: Free Press

Easton, D. (1991) The division, integration, and transfer of knowledge. In D. Easton & C.S. Scelling (eds) *Divided Knowledge* Newbury Park: Sage, pp. 7–36

Edwards, R. (1997) *Changing Places?* London: Routledge

Elliott, J. (ed.) (1993) *Reconstructing Teacher Education* London: Falmer Press

Elton, L. (1992) Research, teaching and scholarship in an expanding higher education system, *Higher Education Quarterly*, 46, 3, pp. 252–268

Elton, L. (1993) University teaching: a professional model for quality. In R. Ellis (ed.) *Quality Assurance for University Teaching* Guildford: OU Press/SRHE

Entwistle, N. (1997) Reconstructing approaches to learning: a response to Webb, *Higher Education*, 33, pp. 213–218

Etzioni, E. (1995) *The Spirit of Community: Rights, Responsibilities and the Communitarian Agenda* London: Falmer Press

Evans, G.R. (2002) *Academics and the Real World* Buckingham: SRHE/Open University Press

Ewell, P.T. (1997) Organising for learning: a point of entry. AAHE. http://www.intime.uni.edu/model/learning/lear.html

Farrugia, C. (1996) A continuing professional development model for quality assurance in higher education, *Quality Assurance in Education*, 4, 2, pp. 28–34

Fincher, C. (2000) *Defining and Appraising Scholarship*. Institute of Higher Education Perspectives. Meigs Hall: University of Georgia

Friedson, E. (1994) *Professionalism Reborn* Chicago: University of Chicago Press

Frost, S.H. & Jean, P.M. (1999) Bridging the disciplines: interdisciplinary discourses and faculty scholarship, *Journal of Higher Education*, 74, 1, pp. 119–149

Fukuyama, F. (1995) *Trust: The Social Virtues and the Creation of Prosperity* Harmondsworth: Penguin

Fullan, M. (1991) *The New Meaning of Educational Change* London: Cassells

Fullan, M. (2002) *Change Forces* London: Routledge

Gadamer, H.G. (1997) *Sanning och metod-1 urval* Göteborg: Daidalos

Gaff, J.G. (1989) The resurgence of interdisciplinary studies, *National Forum*, 69, pp. 4–5

Geiger, R.L. (1993) *Research and Relevant Knowledge: American Research Universities, 1900–1940* New York: Oxford University Press

Gibbins, N. (1998) Scholarship and teaching: the defining conjunction of the university. http://www.uoguelph.ca/atguelph/98-06-03/insight.html

Giddens, A. (1999). Risk and responsibility, *Modern Law Review*, 62, 1, pp. 1–10

Glanville, I. & Houde, S. (2004) The scholarship of teaching: implications for nursing faculty, *Journal of Professional Nursing*, 20, 1, pp. 7–14

Glasgow, N.A. (1997) *A New Curriculum for New Times: A Guide to Student-Centered Problem-Based Learning* Thousand Oaks, CA: Corwin Press

Glassick, C. (1997) *Scholarship in Higher Education* Canberra: HEC

Glassick, C.E., Huber, M.T. & Maeroff, G.I. (1997) *Scholarship Assessed: Evaluation of the Professoriate.* Special Report of the Carnegie Foundation for the Advancement of Teaching. San Francisco: Jossey-Bass

Goel, S. (2004) What is high about higher education? *National Teaching and Learning Forum*, 13, 4

Gosling, D. (2001) Educational development units in the UK – what are they doing five years on?, *International Journal for Academic Development*, 6, 1, pp. 74–90

Grenfell, M. & James, D. (1998) *Bourdieu and Education: Acts of Practical Theory* London: Falmer Press

Grossman, P.L., Wilson, S.N. & Shulman, L.S. (1989) Teachers of substance: subject matter, knowledge for teaching. In M. Reynolds (ed.) *Knowledge Base for Beginning Teachers* New York: Pergamon, pp. 23–36

Grube, G.M.A. (1935) *Plato's Thought* London: Athlone Press

Hahn, R. (1990) What we talk about when we talk teaching. In D. DeZure (ed.) *Learning from Change* Sterling, VA: AAHE/Sterling Publishing, 2000, pp. 11–12

Harre, R. (1998) *The Singular Self* London: Sage

Hativa, N. & Marincovich, M. (eds) (1995) *Disciplinary Differences in Teaching and Learning: Implications for Practice* San Francisco: Jossey-Bass

HEA (2004) Towards a framework of professional development. Consultation paper, Universities UK/SCOP/HEFCE/HEA

Healey, M. (2000) Developing the scholarship of teaching in higher education: a discipline-based approach, *Higher Education Research and Development*, 19, pp. 169–189

Healey, M. (2003) Promoting lifelong professional development in geography education: international perspective on developing the scholarship of teaching in higher education in the twenty first century, *Professional Geographer*, 55, 1, pp. 1–17

HEFCE (2003) *Building Capacity for Change: Research on the Scholarship of Teaching* Bristol: HEFCE

HEFCE (2004) *Centres for Excellence in Teaching and Learning: Invitations to Bid for Funds* Bristol: HEFCE

HEFCE (2004) *Towards a Framework of Professional Teaching Standards* Bristol: HEFCE

Henkel, M. (2000) *Academic Identities and Policy Change in Higher Education* London: Kingsley

Hoare, D., Stanley, G., Kirky, R. & Coaldrake, P. (1995) Risk management. In *Risk Analysis, Perception and Management* London: Royal Society, pp. 135–201

Huber, M.T. (1999) *Disciplinary Styles in the Scholarship of Teaching*. Keynote address, 75th International Symposium on Improving Student Learning. University of York, UK

Huber, M.T. & Morreale, S. (2002) *Disciplinary Styles in the Scholarship of Teaching and Learning: Exploring Common Ground* Washington, DC: AAHE

Humes, W. & Bryce, T. (2001) Scholarship, research and the evidential basis of policy development in education, *British Journal of Educational Studies*, 49, 3, pp. 329–353

Hutchings, P. (1996) *Making Teaching Community Property: A Menu for Peer Collaboration and Peer Review* Washington, DC: AAHE

Hutchings, P. (1998) Defining features and significant functions of course portfolios. Carnegie Foundation

Hutchings, P. & Shulman, L. (1999) The scholarship of teaching: new elaborations, new developments, *Change*, 31, 5, pp. 10–15

ILTHE (2003) *Annual Report 2002/3* York: ILTHE

Inlow, G. (1972) *Values in Transition* London: Wiley and Sons

Jarvis, P. (1992) *Paradoxes of Learning* London: Jossey-Bass

Jarvis, P. (1995) *Adult and Continuing Education* London: Routledge

Jarvis, P. (1998) *The Theory and Practice of Learning* London: Stylus

Jarvis, P. (1999) *The Practitioner-Researcher: Developing Theory from Practice* San Francisco: Jossey-Bass

Jarvis, P. (2002) *The Theory and Practice of Teaching* London: Kogan Page

Jencks, C. & Riesman, D. (1968) *The American Revolution: Rethinking Social Policy* Chicago: University of Chicago Press

Jones, P.C. & Quentin-Merritt, J. (1999) Critical thinking and interdisciplinarity in environmental higher education: the case for epistemological and values awareness, *Journal of Geography in Higher Education*, 23, 3, pp. 349–357

Kant, I. (2002) *Critique of Pure Reason* London: Hackett

Katz, L. & Raths, J. (eds) (1984) *Advances in Teacher Education* Norwood: Ablex

Kember, D. (1997) A reconceptualization of the research into university academics' conceptions of teaching, *Learning and Instruction*, 7, pp. 325–351

Kierkegaard, S. (1940) *Thoughts on Critical Situations in Human Life* (trans. Walter Lowerie) Princeton: Princeton University Press

Kiger, J.C. (1971) Disciplines. In J. Kockelmans (ed.) *Interdisciplinarity and Higher Education* University Park: Pennsylvania State University Press, pp. 52–53

Kockelmans, J.J. (ed.) (1979) Interdisciplinarity? In J. Kockelmans (ed.) *Interdisciplinarity and Higher Education*, University Park: Pennsylvania State University Press, pp. 11–48

Kolb, D.A. (1981) Learning styles and disciplinary differences. In A. Chickering (ed.) *The Modern American College* San Francisco: Jossey-Bass, pp. 232–255

Kreber, C. (1999) A course-based approach to the development of teaching-scholarship: a case study, *Teaching in Higher Education*, 4, pp. 309–325

Kreber, C. (2000) How teaching award winners conceptualise academic work: further thoughts on the meaning of scholarship, *Teaching in Higher Education*, 5, pp. 61–78

Kreber, C. (ed.) (2001) *Scholarship Revisited: Perspectives on the Scholarship of Teaching* San Francisco: Jossey-Bass

Kreber, C. (2002a) Controversy and consensus on the scholarship of teaching, *Studies in Higher Education*, 27, 2, pp. 151–167

Kreber, C. (2002b) *The Scholarship of Teaching: A Comparison of Conceptions Held by Experts and Regular Academic Staff* Edmonton: University of Alberta Press

Kreber, C. (2002c) Teaching excellence, teaching expertise, and the scholarship of teaching, *Innovative Higher Education*, 27, 1, pp. 5–23

Kreber, C. & Cranton, P.A. (2000) Exploring the scholarship of teaching, *Journal of Higher Education*, 71, pp. 476–495

Lamont, M. & Fournier, M. (1992) Introduction. In M. Lamont & M. Fournier (eds) *Cultivating Differences: Symbolic Boundaries and the Making of Inequality* Chicago: University of Chicago Press, pp. 1–20

Larsson, H. (1997) *Intuition* Stockholm: Dialoger

Lave, J. & Wenger, E. (1991) *Situated Learning: Legitimate Peripheral Participation* Cambridge: Cambridge University Press

LeBaron, J.F. (2001) *Rhetoric and Reward in Higher Education.* http://www. Gse.uml.edu/lebaron/Gulbenk010515.htm

Lortie, D. (1975) *Schoolteacher: A Sociological Study* Chicago: University of Chicago Press

Lucas, C.J. (1996) *Crisis in the Academy: Rethinking Higher Education in America* London: Macmillan Press

Luedekke, G. (2003) Professionalising teaching practice in higher education: a study of disciplinary variation and teaching-scholarship, *Studies in Higher Education*, 28, 2, pp. 213–228

Lynch, J., Sheard, J., Carbone, A. & Collins, F. (2002) The scholarship of teaching: risky business in ICT education. Conference paper presented at the Australian Association for Research in Education

Lynton, E. (1995) *Making the Case for Professional Service* Washington, DC: AAHE

Lyotard, J.-P. (1984) *The Postmodern Condition: Knowledge, Theory of Civilisation, Postmodernism and the 20th Century* Minneapolis: University of Minnesota Press

Lyotard, J.-P. (1988) *The Postmodern Condition and the Postmodern Sublime* New York: Columbia University Press

McInnis, C. (1993) *Academic Values under Pressure* Melbourne: CSHE

MacIntyre, A. (1981) *After Virtue: A Study of Moral Theory* London: Duckworth

McWilliam, E. (2004) Changing the academic subject, *Studies in Higher Education*, 29, 2, pp. 151–163

Marcus, G.E. (1998) *Ethnography Through Thick and Thin* Princeton, NJ: Princeton University Press

Martin, B. (1998) *Tied Knowledge and Power in Higher Education.* http://www.uow.edu.au/arts/sts/bmartin/pubs/98tk/

Marx, L. (1989) A case for interdisciplinary thinking, *National Forum*, 69, pp. 8–11

Mawditt, R. (1998) Lest we forget, *Higher Education Policy*, 11, pp. 323–330

Menand, L. (ed.) (1996) *The Future of Academic Freedom* London: University of Chicago Press

Menges, R. & Weimer, M. (1996) *Teaching on Solid Ground* San Francisco: Jossey-Bass

Metzger, W.P. (1987) The academic profession in the USA. In B. Clark (ed.) *The Academic Profession: National, Disciplinary and International Settings* Berkeley: University of California Press, pp. 123–208

Miles, T. (1989) *Nebraska Policy Choices, 1989: Education* Lincoln, NE: Nebraska Press

Morehead, J.M. & Shedd, P.J. (1996) Students' interviews: a vital role in the scholarship of teaching, *Innovative Higher Education*, 20, 4, pp. 261–269

Neumann, R., Parry, S. & Becher, T. (2002) Teaching and learning in their disciplinary contexts: a conceptual analysis, *Studies in Higher Education*, 27, 4, pp. 405–417

Newell, W.H. & Klein, J.T. (1999) Interdisciplinarity studies into the 21st century, *Journal of Education*, 45, 1, pp. 152–169

Newman, J.H. (1996) *The Idea of a University* (ed. F.M.Turner) New Haven: Yale University Press

Nicholls, G.M. (2000) Professional development, teaching, and lifelong learning: is there a connection? *International Journal of Lifelong Learning and Adult Education*, 19, 4, pp. 157–174

Nicholls, G.M. (2001) *Professional Development in Higher Education: New Dimensions and Directions* London: Kogan Page

Nicholls, G.M. (2002) *Developing Teaching and Learning in Higher Education* London: RoutledgeFalmer

Nicholls, G.M. & Jarvis, P. (2002) Teaching, learning and the changing landscape. In P. Jarvis (ed.) *The Theory and Practice of Teaching* London: Kogan Page

Nixon, J. (2001) 'Not without dust and heat': the moral bases of the 'new' academic professionalism, *British Journal of Educational Studies*, 49, 2, pp. 173–186

Nixon, J., Marks, A., Rowland, S. & Walker, M. (2001) Towards a new academic professionalism: a manifesto of hope, *British Journal of Sociology of Education*, 22, 2, pp. 227–244

Oakley, F. (1995) Scholarship and teaching: a matter of mutual support. American Council of Learned Societies Occasional Paper No.32. http://www.acls.org/op32.htp

Ornstein, A.C. & Levine, D.U. (1981) *An Introduction to the Foundations of Education* Boston: Houghton Mifflin

Özesmi, Y. (1999) *Metadisciplinarity, Scholars and Scholarship.* http://env.erciyes.edu.tr/abstracts/metadisciplinary.htm

Palmer, P.J. (1998) *The Courage to Teach* San Francisco: Jossey-Bass

Parks, M.R. (1997) Where does scholarship begin? Address to the National Communication Association, Chicago http://acjournal.org/holdings/vol1/Iss2/special/parks.htm

Parsons, T. (1968) The professions. In *The International Encyclopedia of Social Science* New York: Macmillan

Pascarella, E.T. & Terenzini, P.T. (1991) *How College Affects Students: Findings and Insights from Twenty Years of Research* San Francisco: Jossey-Bass

Passmore, J. (1980) *The Philosophy of Teaching* London: Duckworth

Paulsen, M.B. & Feldman, K. (1995) Towards a reconceptualisation of scholarship: a human action system with functional imperatives, *Journal of Higher Education*, 66, pp. 615–641

Pelikan, J. (1992) *The Idea of a University: A Re-examination* New Haven and London: Yale University Press

Perley, J.E. (1997) Tenure remains vital to academic freedom. American Association of University Professors. http://www.aaup.org/jeped44.htm

Peterson, M.W. & Spencer, M.G. (1990) Understanding academic culture and climate. In W.G. Tierney (ed.) *Assessing Academic Climate and Culture*, New Directions of International Research No. 68. San Francisco: Jossey-Bass

Pfnister, A.O. (1969) The influence of departmental or disciplinary perspectives on curricular formation. In J.R. Davis, *Interdisciplinarity Courses and Team Teaching: New Arrangements for Learning* Phoenix: Oryx Press

Preece, J. & Houghton, A. (2000) *Nurturing Social Capital in Excluded Communities* Aldershot: Ashgate

Prosser, M., Ramsden, P., Trigwell, K. & Martin, E. (2003) Dissonance in experience of teaching and its relation to the quality of student learning, *Studies in Higher Education*, 28, 1, pp. 37–48

Prosser, M., Trigwell, K. & Taylor, P. (1994) A phenomenographic study of academics' conceptions of science learning and teaching, *Learning and Instruction*, 4, pp. 217–231

Prosser, M. & Trigwell, K. (1997) Relations between perceptions of the teaching environment and approaches to teaching, *British Journal of Educational Psychology*, 67, 1, pp. 25–35

Ramsden, P. (1992) *Learning to Teach in Higher Education* London: Routledge

Randel, D.M. (1997) The university in the future. http://iotu.uchicago.edu/randel.html

Rankin, H.D. (1983) *Sophists, Socratics and Cynics* New Jersey: Croom-Helm

Reybold, E. (2001) Knowing through culture: epistemological developments as redefinition of self, *International Journal of Curriculum and Instruction*, 3, 2, pp. 1–7

Reybold, E. (2003) Pathways to the professorate: the development of faculty identity in education, *Innovative Higher Education*, 27, 4 (summer)

Rice, E. (1996) Making a place for the New American Scholar. AAHE Forum on Faculty Roles and Rewards, Washington, DC

Rice, R. (1992) Towards a broader conception of scholarship: the American context. In T. Whitson & R. Geiger (eds) *Research and Higher Education: The United Kingdom and the United States* Buckingham: SRHE/OU Press

Richlin, L. (2001) Scholarly teaching and the scholarship of teaching. In C. Kreber (ed.) *Revisiting Scholarship: Identifying and Implementing the Scholarship of Teaching*. New Directions for Teaching and Learning, No. 86 San Francisco: Jossey-Bass

Ringel, R.L. (2000) Managing change in higher education, *Assessment and Accountablity Forum* (fall)

Ringer, F. (1992) *Field of Knowledge: French Academic Culture in Comparative Perspective* Cambridge: Cambridge University Press

Rogoff, B. (1984) Introduction: thinking and learning in social context. In B. Rogoff & J. Lave (eds) *Everyday Cognition: Its Development in Social Contexts* Cambridge, MA: Harvard University Press, pp. 1–8

Rothblatt, S. (1997) *The Modern University and its Discontents: The Fate of Newman's Legacies in Britain and America* Cambridge: Cambridge University Press

Rowland, S. (2002) Overcoming fragmentation in professional life: the challenge for academic development, *Higher Education Quarterly*, 56, 1, pp. 52–64

Roy, R. (1979) Interdisciplinary science on campus. In J. Kockelmans (ed.) *Interdisciplinarity and Higher Education* University Park: Pennsylvania State University Press, pp. 161–196

Ruscio, K.P. (1986) Bridging specialisations: reflections from biology and political science, *Review of Higher Education*, 10, pp. 29–45

Russell, B. (1956) *Logic and Knowledge* London: Allen & Unwin

Santoro, N. (2003) Caught up in the teaching–training divide: confusing professional identities, *Studies in Continuing Education*, 25, 2, pp. 211–224

Schön, D. (1983) *The Reflective Practitioner* San Francisco: Jossey-Bass
Schön, D. (1991) *Educating the Reflective Practitioner: Towards a New Design for Teaching and Learning in the Professions* San Francisco: Jossey-Bass
Schwab, J. (1964) Structures of the disciplines: meanings and significance. In G.W. Ford & L. Pugno (eds) *The Structure of Knowledge and the Curriculum* Chicago: Rand McNally, pp. 6–30
Senge, P. (1990) *The Fifth Discipline: The Art of Practice of the Learning Organisation* New York: Doubleday
Senge, P. (2000) *Rethinking the Fifth Discipline* London: Sage
Shain, F. & Gleeson, D. (1999) Under new management: changing conceptions of teacher professionalism and policy in the further education sector, *Journal of Educational Policy*, 14, 4, pp. 445–462
Shulman, L.S. (1987) Knowledge and teaching, *Harvard Educational Review*, 57, pp. 1–22
Shulman, L.S. (1993) Teaching as community property: putting an end to pedagogic solitude, *Change* (Nov./Dec.), pp. 6–7
Shulman, L.S. (1997) Disciplines of inquiry in education: a new overview. In R.M. Jaeger (ed.) *Complementary Methods for Research in Education* Washington, DC: American Educational Research Association, pp. 3–30
Shulman, L.S. (1998) Course anatomy: the dissection and analysis of knowledge through teaching. In P. Hutchings (ed.) *The Course Portfolio* Washington, DC: American Association for Higher Education
Shulman, L.S. (1999) Taking learning seriously, *Change*, 31, 4, pp. 10–17
Smart, J.C., Feldman, K.A. & Ethington, C.A. (2000) *Academic Disciplines: Holland's Theory and the Study of College Students and Faculty* Nashville, TN: Vanderbilt University Press
Smart, R.L., Drimmel, R., Latlanz, M. and Binney, J.J. (1998) *Nature*, 392, p. 471
Smeby, J.C. (1996) Disciplinary differences in university teaching, *Studies in Higher Education*, 21, pp. 69–79
Smith, P. (1990) *Killing the Spirit: Higher Education in America* New York: Viking Penguin
Snow, R.E. (1989) Toward assessment of cognitive and conative structures in learning, *Educational Researcher*, 18, 9, pp. 8–14. http://www.aera.net/pubs/er/"\t"_blank
Stilwell, F. (2003) Higher education, commercial criteria and economic incentives, *Journal of Higher Education Policy and Management*, 25, 1, pp. 51–62
Sullivan, J. (2003) Scholarship and spirituality. In D. Carr & J. Haldane (eds) *Spirituality, Philosophy and Education* London: RoutledgeFalmer
Swoboda, W.W. (1979) Disciplines and interdisciplinarity: a historical perspective. In J. Kockelmans (ed.) *Interdisciplinarity and Higher Education* University Park: University of Pennsylvania Press, pp. 49–92
Sykes, C. (1989) *Prof Scam: Professors and the Demise of Higher Education* New York: St. Martin's Press
Teichler, U. (1998) Current agendas and priorities in higher education policy

research: an international view. International conference, Canberra. http://fehps.une.edu.an/x/ANHER/public/teichler/teichler.html

Terenzini, P.T., Rendon, L.I., Upcraft, M.L., Millar, S.B., Allison, K.W., Gregg, P.L. & Jalomo, R. (1994) The transition to college: diverse students, divers stories *Research in Higher Education*, 57, p. 73

Terenzini, P.T., Springer, L., Pascarella, E.T. & Nora, A. (1995) Influences affecting the development of students' critical thinking skills, *Research in Higher Education*, 36, pp. 29–39

Thompson, J.B. (1991) Editor's introduction. In P. Bourdieu, *Language and Symbolic Power* Cambridge: Polity

Thomson, D. (ed.) (1996) *The Oxford Modern Dictionary*, 2nd edn. Oxford: Oxford University Press

Tierney, W.G. & Rhoads, R.A. (1994) Faculty socialisation as cultural process: a mirror of institutional commitment. ASHE-ERIC Higher Education Report No. 93–6. Washington, DC

Trigwell, K. (2001) Judging university teaching, *International Journal for Academic Development*, 6, 1, pp. 65–73

Trigwell, K., Martin, E., Benjamin, J. and Prosser, M. (2000) Scholarship of teaching: a model, *Higher Education Research and Development*, 19, 2, pp. 155–168

Universities UK (2004) *Towards a Framework of Professional Teaching Standards* London: Universities UK

Vlastos, G. (1971) *The Philosophy of Socrates: A Collection of Critical Essays* New York: Anchor Press

Wann, M. (1995) *Building Social Capital* London: IPPR

Whewell, W. (1840) *Philosophy of the Inductive Sciences* London: British Library Archives

Whitsitt, J. In S. Barnes (ed.) (1990) *Professors and Scholarship: A Selection of Essays from the Chronicle of Higher Education* Lampeter: Edwin Mellen Press

Wilson, E.O. (1998) *Consilience: The Unity of Knowledge* New York: Alfred Knopf

Winston, G. (1994) The decline of undergraduate teaching: moral failure or market pressures? In D. DeZure (ed.) *Learning from Change* Sterling, VA: AAHE/Sterling Publishing, 2000, pp. 41–42

Wittgenstein, L. (1953) *Philosophical Investigations* Oxford: Basil Blackwell

# Index

AAHE *see* American Association for Higher Education
*Academic Disciplines* Smart, J.C. 86–8
academic learning: priority debate 29; professional image, criteria 116–17; risk 123–30; scholarship 57–8, 66
Allen, K.E. 18
American Association for Higher Education (AAHE) 100
Andresen, L.W. 52, 105
Archer, M. 95
Aristotle 25, 38, 41
Australia: CATLHE 100; scholarship of teaching 103–8

Badley, G. 40, 41, 43, 46, 106
Bamber, V. 45
Barnett, R. 29–30, 45, 77, 98, 124–5
Bauman, Z. 95, 96
Baxter, M.M. 89
Becher, T. 43, 74–7
Beck, U. 95
Bennis, W. 130
bicycle, meaning 36
Biglan, A. 74–5
Birch, W. 44–5
Birgerstam, P. 122–3

Blake, N. 45
book structure 5–8
bottom-up approach 100–3
boundaries, disciplines 83
Bourdieu, P. 19, 83; symbolic culture concept 55–7
Bourdieu's notions 64–6
Bowers, J. 85
Boyer, E. 29, 36, 38–41; analysis of scholarship 117; notions 56–7; research versus teaching 51–2; teaching 48
Boyer's scholarship reconsidered 58–9
Braxton, J. 51
Breakwell, G. 42, 94
Bryce, T. 46

car, meaning example 3
Carnegie Academy for the Scholarship of Teaching and Learning (CASTL) 104–5
Carnegie foundation 31, 44
CASTL *see* Carnegie Academy for the Scholarship of Teaching and Learning
CATLHE *see* Committee for the Advancement of Teaching and Learning in Higher Education

Centres for Excellence in Teaching
    and Learning (CETL) 101
CETL *see* Centres for Excellence in
    Teaching and Learning
Chait, R.P. 28
challenge of the future 113–32
challenges, scholarship roles 94
change barriers 89–91
change understanding, scholarship
    role 130–2
changing concepts 13–14, 130–2
Cobbs, P. 85
Committee for the Advancement of
    Teaching and Learning in Higher
    Education (CATLHE) 100
community of scholars 76
competitive influence 82–3
complete scholar view 16
the concept, reconsideration 47–9
*Confessions*(Tolstoy) 26
consensus, need 108–10
*consilience* concept 13
core values challenge 135–6
Craft, A. 43
Cross, P. 79
cultural capital 62–6
Cummings, R.J. 134
curriculum disciplines 86–9

Davis, J.R. 74
Dearing Report 106
definitions: policy driven 46;
    scholarship 42–4, 57–8
Dewey, J. 120–1
dilemmas, higher education
    community 128
disciplines 75–7; academic power
    90–1; barriers to change 89–91;
    boundaries 83; challenging the
    power 73–91; competitive
    influence 82–3; consideration
    74–8; curriculum 86–9; fear
    notions 82–3; groupings 74–5;
    institution models 101–2;

meaning 73–4; power of expertise
    88–9; power of specialization 76;
    students' learning 86–9; teaching
    learning issues 80–3; tradition
    aspects 87
Dixon, N. 132
Downie, R. 98–100
*driving* concept 47
Duderstadt, J.J. 128, 131
Durkheim, E. 77

education ideals 22–7
education scholarship, Socratic
    approach 23–4
Edwards, R. 120
Elton, L. 47–8, 103
England, higher education
    dilemmas 128
epistemology 14–15, 84–5
Etzioni, E. 62
Evans, G.R. 22
Ewell, P.T. 123
excellence problem 49–51

fear influence 82–3
*Fields of knowledge* (Ringer) 11
Fincher, C. 22
Fox, - 128–9
France, German university model 12
FTDL *see* Fund for the Development
    of Teaching and Learning
Fukumaya, F. 62–3
Fullan, M. 130
Fund for the Development of
    Teaching and Learning (FTDL)
    101

Gadamer, H.G. 124
Germany: research university model
    29–30; scholarship of teaching
    104; university education model
    11–12
Gibbins, N. 15–16
Giddens, A. 95

Glassick, C.E. 39–41
Gosling, D. 103
*gunpoint scholarship* 30

*habitus* 19, 42, 83
Hamack, Adolf von, research
    mission 11–12
HEA *see* Higher Education
    Academy
Healey, M. 100, 109
HEFCE *see* Higher Education
    Funding Council for England
Henkel, M. 101
higher education: dilemmas 128;
    *see also* research led higher
    education
Higher Education Academy (HEA)
    31; national standards framework
    49
Higher Education Bill (2004), UK 29
Higher Education Funding Council
    for England (HEFCE) 46
historical arguments 38–42
historical concepts, scholarship 9–31
Hobbes, - 135
Holland's theory 86–7
Huber, M.T. 43, 78–9, 80, 101
Humes, W. 46
Hutchings, P. 41–2

ideal teacher-scholar 115
ideals 22–7
ILT *see* Institute for Learning and
    Teaching
ILTHE *see* Institute for Learning
    and Teaching in Higher
    Education
individual autonomy and values
    102–3
initiatives 35–54; scholarship 127
Inlow, G. 42
Institute for Learning and Teaching
    in Higher Education (ILTHE)
    50

Institute for Learning and Teaching
    (ILT) 56, 63–4
international perspective 93–110;
    scholarship of teaching 103–8

Jarvis, P. 17, 20–1, 52, 132

Kant, I. 26
Kennedy, Donald, Stanford
    University 31
Kierkegaard, S. 26–7
Kiger, J.C. 74
knowing and learning, academic
    perspective 120–3
knowledge tradition 76
Kockelmans, J.J. 74
Kolb, D.A. 74
Kreber, C. 104
Kreber, K. 50–1
Kreber model, scholarship of
    teaching 61

Larsson, H. 124
Lave, J. 85
learners' perspective 37
learning and rationality, university
    education 26
learning teaching issues, disciplines
    80–3
LeBaron, J.F. 28
Locke, John 3
Lortie, D. 122
Lucas, C.J. 29–30
Lueddeke, G. 101, 103
Lynton, E. 16
Lyotard, J.-P. 21

McInnis, C. 43, 101
MacIntyre, A. 18–19
McWilliam, E. 106, 107
Martin, B. 88, 90
Mawditt, R. 96
Menand, L. 101–2
Menges, R. 39

Metzger, W.P. 76
Mill, John Stuart, scholarship notion 38
mode of learning 84
Morreau, S. 43

national standards framework, Higher Education Academy 49
new initiatives, scholarship 127
Newman, J.H. 9–11
Nixon, J. 97, 102
numerical strength, need for consensus 108–10

objectivism 84–5
obstacles, scholarship teaching research 125–6
Orwell, George 10
Özesmi, Y. 79–80

Palmer, P.J. 80–3, 88
paradigm shifts 134
Parks, M.R. 21–2
Parsons, T. 116
Passmore, J. 48
pedagogical content knowledge 60
Pelikan, J. 11
Pew Scholars National Fellowship program 104–5
philosophical arguments 12, 38–42
*Philosophical Investigations* (Wittgenstein) 53
Plato's *Republic* 23
polemic scholarship 57–8
policies, UK 37
policy 35–54; driven definitions 46; power influences 33–110
power, disciplines 86–9
process definition 45–6
*Prof Scam* (Sykes) 11
professional standards 136–7
professional values 56
professionalism and scholarship 97–100

quality assurance 98
quotations, terminology 69

RAE *see* Research Assessment Exercise
Rankin, H.D. 24
recent influences 136–7
reconceptualization need 35–54; academics' role 53–4
*Republic* (Plato) 23
research: methodology 66–7; teaching conflict 29–30, 77–8; teaching models 124–5; teaching tensions 77–8; university goal 11–12
Research Assessment Exercise (RAE) 107, 116
research led higher education 14; teaching issue 114–18
research scholarship models, *see also* scholarship of teaching
Reybold, E. 85
Rice, E. 16
Rice, R. 41, 115–16
Richilin, L. 44
Ringel, R.L. 130
Ringer, F. 11
risk analysis, academic 128–30
risk society, impact on values 95–6
Rogoff, B. 85
Roy, R. 74
Ruscio, K.P. 78
Russell, B. 53

Santaro, N. 96
scholars: Coleridge's view 22; lexical definition 9
scholarship: basic principles 68; Boyer's key roles 59–60; challenge 3–8, 113–32; challenges 94; challenging 133–4; changing concept 13–14; conflict 27–30; context 3–5, 56–7, 118; definitions 38, 48–9, 67–8; diagram of

elements 119–20; disciplinary
  styles 78–80; four forms 59–60;
  Greek definition 9; historical
  concepts 9–31; holistic approach
  51; hostage to fortune 133–41;
  ideals of education 22–7;
  implications for professionalism
  93–110; interpretation 36–7; key
  roles 117; meaning within
  disciplines 68–9; means of
  challenging core values 135–6;
  misuses 55–6; next move 30–1;
  practice research relationship
  18–21; purpose 18–21; recent
  influences 136–7;
  reconceptualizing need 35–54;
  research teaching models 124–5;
  research versus teaching 51–2;
  role 118–20; scholars 21–2;
  teaching research obstacles 125–6
scholarship aspects: discovery 59;
  four forms 59–60; integration
  59–60; learning activity 14–18;
  model 48–9; Socratic approach
  23–4
*Scholarship Assessed* (Glassick) 39
scholarship process, concepts
  conflict 50
*Scholarship Reconsidered* (Boyer) 36
scholarship of teaching 36, 54,
  55–73; academics' perceptions 66;
  Australia 103–8; individual
  influences 100–3; international
  perspective 103–8; models 40–2;
  perspectives on meaning 108–10;
  Trigwell model 60–1
Schön, D. 124
Schulman, L.S. 15, 37, 41–2, 79, 89;
  research versus teaching 52;
  scholarship definition 57–8
Schwab, J. 80
Senge, P. 18, 132
Smart, J.C. 86–8
Snow, R.E. 76, 77–8

social capital 62–3
Socrates 23–4
specialization, increases 76–8
Stanford University 31
Stilwell, F. 96
students learning 86–9
Sullivan, J. 42, 95, 100, 107
Sykes, C. 11
symbolic capital 64–6
synoptic capacity 60

table meaning example 39–40
teaching: Greek view 38; learning
  issues 80–3; research conflict
  29–30; research scholarship
  models 124–5; research issues
  77–8
tenure challenge, USA 28
Terenzini, P.T. 89
terminology concepts 3, 69–72
terminology understandings,
  scholarship of teaching 3, 69–72
*The Future of Higher Education* (Dfes)
  49, 107
*The Idea of a University: A re-
  examination* (Pelikan) 11
*The idea of a University* (Newman)
  9–11
'the scholarship of teaching' 5, 29
'theory of practice' (Bourdieu) 19
theory and practice categorization,
  Jarvis 20–1
Thompson, J.B. 19
Thomson, D. 9
Tolstoy, Leo. 26
Trigwell, K. 40, 104
Trigwell model, scholarship of
  teaching 60–1
'true knowledge' 22
'tyranny of academic tenure' 28

United Kindom, government
  initiatives 118
United Kingdom: Higher Education

Academy 31; Higher Education Bill (2004) 29; scholarship of teaching 103–8
United States: Carnegie foundation 31; German philosophy model 12; scholarship of teaching 29, 103–8; 'tyranny of academic tenure' 28
universities: German model 11–12; learning and rationality 26; research goal 11–12

values, defining scholarship 42–4

Wann, M. 62
ways of knowing 84–6
Weismer *see* Menges
Wenger, E. *see* Lave, J.
Whewell, W. 13
Whitsitt, J. 38
Winston, G. 28
Wittgenstein, L. 3–4, 39, 53, 117